SLOcals Only

EPIC *Adventures in San Luis Obispo and the Surrounding Central Coast*

JARED FRIEDMAN

SLOcals Only

EPIC Adventures in San Luis Obispo and the Surrounding Central Coast

First Edition

Written & Photographed by Jared Friedman

© 2022 Just Say Nomad Press

ISBN: 978-1-7373457-0-1

All rights reserved. No part of this book may be translated or reproduced in any form, except for brief extracts by a reviewer for the purposes of a review, without the prior written permission of the author, which you may obtain by e-mailing slocalsonly1@gmail.com.

Notice a change or mistake while using this guide? If so, please send an e-mail to slocalsonly1@gmail.com. Your input will make future editions even better!

All text and photography by the author, except where noted.

Edited by Taylor Friedman.

All recommendations, including those for sights, restaurants, shops, hotels, and activities, are based on the author's individual judgment. No payment, free goods, or services were exchanged for any positive coverage.

Legal Disclaimer: Although every effort was made to verify the accuracy of the information contained herein at press time, the author and publisher do not assume and hereby disclaim any liability to any party for any loss or damage caused by errors, omissions, or any potential travel disruption due to labor or financial difficulty, whether such errors or omissions result from negligence, accident, or any other source. If any of the activities are beyond your capabilities, do not attempt them. Maps for many hikes and adventures were prepared with the best-known information at the time of publication, but accuracy and completeness are not guaranteed and readers are encouraged to supplement the information in this book with their own research for up-to-date conditions.

See SLO Map in back of the book

Contents

Introduction		6
Brief History of San Luis Obispo		8
Best Of (in no particular order)		10
Itineraries		11
Precautions		13
1.	SLO City Tour and Cerro San Luis	14
2.	Bishop Peak	26
3.	High School Hill (Bowden Ranch) and Reservoir Canyon	30
4.	Southwest Bike Loop to Avila	35
5.	Southeast Bike Loop: SLO – Arroyo Grande – Pismo Beach – SLO	42
6.	Tri-Tip Challenge	48
7.	Mountain Bike West Cuesta Ridge and Down Poly Canyon	53
8.	Western Bike Loop to Los Osos and Morro Bay	58
9.	Big Sur in a Day	65
10.	Big Sur North	75
11.	Big Sur South	84
12.	San Simeon Day Trip	95
13.	Cambria and Harmony	104
14.	Cayucos and Estero Bluffs	115
15.	Morro Bay City Tour and Urban Hike	124
16.	Morro Rock to Cayucos (And Back)	133
17.	Morro Bay Water Sports and Beach Walk/Run	137
18.	Montaña de Oro (MDO) - The Bluff Trail	141
19.	A Day in the Sahara: MDO Sandspit Beach	149
20.	Montaña De Oro – Summit to Sea	153
21.	Mountain Biking in Montaña De Oro	160
22.	Paso Robles Region	166
23.	Wildflowers off 58	191
24.	Inner Child – Adventure for Kids of All Ages	199

25.	Ontario Ridge Trail (Sycamore Crest) to Pirate's Cave and Pirate's Cove	211
26.	Pismo Preserve	215
27.	Relax and Reflect in Pismo and Avila	222
28.	Pismo Surfing and Kayaking	226
29.	Arroyo Grande and Lopez Lake	229
30.	The Santa Ynez Valley Loop	236
31.	Los Alamos and Buellton	241
32.	Los Olivos and Santa Ynez	246
33.	Solvang	255
34.	Lompoc and Vandenberg	261
35.	Santa Maria and Orcutt	272
36.	Train Ride to Santa Barbara	281
37.	Christmas on the Central Coast	293
About the Author		299

See large version of SLO map in back of book

Introduction

Welcome to what many consider the most beautiful part of the most beautiful state: San Luis Obispo and the surrounding Central Coast in California. In this book, you will get to know the best of this relatively undeveloped area. Located 3.5 hours north of Los Angeles and south of San Francisco, the region is buffered from California's two major population centers, leaving it much more naturally beautiful. Bonus — no traffic! This is the California you thought only your grandparents were lucky enough to experience.

The trips you'll read about in these pages assume you will be starting in San Luis Obispo, abbreviated SLO and pronounced "slow." The focus will be adventures you can do in one day, plus several that you can turn into overnighters. You'll be introduced not just to the top tourist haunts, but to the places where locals eat, shop, and explore. You'll be able to get out, enjoy, and connect with your environment via healthy, active experiences that bring excitement to your life, ideally in the most sustainable way possible. That means less driving, more exercise, eating local food, and supporting local businesses where the passion of the owners shines through.

Like all good adventures, you will be given plenty of choices for the entire day. This is not just a book of hikes; it is a book that gives you options for what you can do before, after, and during whichever physical activity you choose, so that you don't have to spend a bunch of time planning and scheduling your day. You can simply grab this book and go!

Additionally, in almost every section, I present options to make your visit even more adventurous. Instead of your basic, run-of-the-mill hike that you might file under "nice but forgettable," an "**EPIC**" option for an adventure might include a hike, wading through water, dipping your head in a waterfall, getting a little bit lost, finding a new great place to eat, and ending your day with sore legs and lifelong memories.

You will see a few key phrases throughout the book that signify some of the best sights and ways to save money. Use the legend below so you don't miss anything:

EPIC: Kick your adventure up a notch.
Killer Views: Views that will make your jaw drop.
***SLOcals Only* Pro Tip:** Usually highlights a way to save time, money, or otherwise hack what non-SLOcals might be doing.

As you enjoy your time on the Central Coast, I'll make one request: Please do your part to make the places you go even better than you found them, even if it's simply picking up a piece of trash on each hike. I thank you for helping keep the Central Coast beautiful, and so do all future adventurers.

Finally, only you know your own fitness and safety threshold. Conditions change all the time in the outdoors, so while a hike could have been perfectly safe when I wrote about it, a storm could have washed it out and made it insanely dangerous. If conditions don't lead you to believe you will get through the adventure unscathed, turn the page and move on to the next adventure. A great tale is only great if you're around to tell it!

So, open your mind, strap on some good shoes, flip to any page in this book, and get ready to have some fun. Enjoy your time in SLO, which, with this guide in hand, will be nothing short of **EPIC**! Let's get going!

Special thanks to those who helped make this book a reality. It couldn't have been done without my adventurous wife Brooke and our little adventurers Wren and Genevieve. Thanks also to Taylor for your many days and nights helping make this book better in every way possible.

Brief History of San Luis Obispo

If you're like me, you get annoyed with guidebooks where a quarter of the weight is dedicated to history. That's why this section is intentionally short. This book is meant to aid you in getting out and exploring, not learning about everyone and everything that came before you. However, *some* knowledge of local history typically enhances adventures, so in addition to the information below, you'll still get a little history in many of the chapters.

San Luis Obispo is home to just under 50,000 people, and SLO County has a population of approximately 270,000. Founded in 1772 around the Mission San Luis Obispo de Tolosa, SLO is one of California's oldest communities. Originally inhabited by the Chumash people, the area began its movement toward westernization as the Spanish made their push into California. After Mexico's independence from Spain, the area was split into ranchos where livestock and especially cattle were raised. Due to drought, the Gold Rush, and the United States' defeat of Mexico in the Mexican-American War, the area shifted from being primarily a cattle industry to having a broader agricultural focus, which is what you will currently see on display as you travel past the open spaces throughout the county.

There have been some interesting characters along the way who have left their mark on SLO County. Most notable is William Randolph Hearst, whose construction of Hearst Castle in San Simeon caused a ripple effect of development across the county. Alex Madonna and the Madonna family, with their eclectic taste, are the people behind the hard-to-miss, centrally located Madonna Inn. Then there are those who are lesser known but equally influential, like former City Councilman Jerry Reiss. In 1990, he passed an ordinance that banned smoking in all indoor public areas, including bars and restaurants. This made SLO the first municipality anywhere to pass such a ban, and it has been copied throughout the world. In 1982, the city also forbade the construction of "drive-through" businesses. I firmly believe this helps small businesses survive and is the reason our town isn't inundated with fast-food restaurants. Here's something you don't hear every day: "Well done, politicians!"

Many believe that part of SLO's charm has been its slow and even anti-development approach. Makes "SLO" a pretty fitting nickname, don't you think? And with a relatively low crime rate, low unemployment, great weather, great schools, the world-class university Cal Poly San Luis Obispo, countless outdoor activities, proximity to the ocean, and expanding direct flight options, SLO routinely makes "Best Of" lists for places to live. In 2011, Oprah named it "America's Happiest City." In 2016, the Gallup-Healthways Well-Being Index, which ranks 190 metropolitan areas by the well-being of their residents, put SLO County in the Top 10. In 2018, Livability.com named it a Top 20 city in the U.S.

Given the beauty and ever-growing list of things to do in SLO, the history of this area is no doubt just being written.

A final note before we get into the adventures: In 2019, the city passed an "Open Space Regulation" that says hikes are only open one hour before sunrise to one hour after sunset. While some will insist this is so humans don't disrupt nature's plentiful nocturnal creatures, others will loudly complain that this is directed at the students who were partying on Bishop Peak. Not much beats a great sunrise or sunset, and adventures that partake in this phenomenon are automatically kicked up a few notches on the **EPIC** scale — but just keep in mind the hour buffer.

Best Of (in no particular order)

Best Walk: The Bluffs Trail in Montaña de Oro
Best Views: Bishop Peak in SLO
Best Calf Burner in SLO: High School Hill
Best Otherworldly Feeling: Sand Spit in Montaña de Oro
Best One-Day Trip: Big Sur
Best Easy SLO Picnic Sunset: Terrace Hill in SLO
Best Dinner Sunset on a Warm Evening: Mersea's in Avila
Best Cafe to Get Work Done: Kreutzberg in SLO
Grossest: Bubblegum Alley in SLO
Most Relaxing: Sandlewood Spa in Oceano
Most Blubber: Elephant Seal Lookout at Piedras Blancas
Best Chillaxing While Kayaking: Morro Bay
Most Extreme Opulence: Hearst Castle in San Simeon
Best Place You Have to See for Yourself: Madonna Inn men's bathroom in SLO
Best Beach to Have Lots of Space to Yourself: Morro Strand in Cayucos
Best Steakhouse: Jocko's in Nipomo
Best Farmers' Market: San Luis Obispo on Thursday nights
Most Beautiful Sunset From a Winery: Calcareous in Paso Robles
Best Way to Spend New Year's Day: Polar bear dip in Cayucos
Best Long Walk on the Beach: Morro Bay to Cayucos
Best Medium Difficulty Hike with Ocean Views: Pismo Preserve
Most Memorable Cake: A slice from the Madonna Inn in SLO
Best Pastry: Morning bun from Scout in SLO
Best Bread: Bob's Well Bread in Los Alamos
Best Wine and Cupcake Pairing: Saarlos and Sons in Los Olivos
Best Indoor Climbing: The Pad in SLO
Best Cocktail: Sidecar in SLO
Best Brewery on a Sunny Day: Barrelhouse in Paso Robles
Best Outdoor Music: Vina Robles in Paso Robles

Itineraries

1 Day: Bring picnic fixings and start your day bright and early with a coffee and morning bun from Scout or a meal from Linneae's Cafe. Head north on a beautiful road trip on Highway 1. Tour Hearst Castle (prior reservations are a must) then have lunch while overlooking the ocean at Hearst Ranch Winery (reservation a must on weekends). Go north for a few minutes to watch the elephant seals by Piedras Blancas. Making your way back south, stop for a stroll along Moonstone Beach in Cambria. For a great seafood dinner, head to the Sea Chest Oyster Bar and Seafood Restaurant (cash only, get there early) or go to the beach town of Cayucos and take a great sandwich from Cayucos Sausage to the beach for an ocean sunset. Don't forget the Brown Butter Cookies. Finish your day back in SLO with drinks at one of the many spots downtown and make sure to grab a cocktail at Sidecar.

2 Days: Do the 1 Day itinerary first. On day 2, pack some snacks and grab some doughnuts at SloDoCo. Hike 1 of the big three peaks in town; Bishop Peak, Cerro San Luis or High School Hill. Grab a sandwich at Lincoln Market or High Street Deli. Head to Morro Bay and rent kayaks or stand-up paddleboards. Stroll along the boardwalk. Have dinner with a sunset over the water at Tognazzini's Dockside Too or Giovanni's Fish Market or grab your dinner to go and drive up Black Mountain to get one of the best sunset views on the Central Coast. Head to The Siren or Stax Bar to finish off your day.

3-4 Days: With a few extra days you can explore several more jewels of the Central Coast. Do the spectacular stretch of Highway 1 to the magical area of Big Sur (see adventures #9, 10 and 11). Surround yourself with towering oak trees and find your new favorite wine among more than 300 wineries in one of the largest wine regions in the world in Paso Robles (adventure #22). Or, grab a bike and cycle your way past stunning rolling hills and catch some killer ocean views (adventures #4, 5, 7, 8 and 21).

5-10 Days: With 5 days or more, you will really get to experience the beauty in every direction from SLO. During these days, enjoy the perfect air of the Pacific and maybe spot a whale or dolphins along the Bluff Trail in Montana de Oro, do a beach stroll and grab clam chowder at Pismo Beach and walk/run/bike the Bob Jones Trail to Avila Beach. Go to one of the many farmer's markets in the region, especially the SLO farmer's market that is held every Thursday evening of the year. Further afield, head south for outstanding wine, food, Dutch charm and ostrich along the Santa Ynez Loop. Perhaps go a little further south to enjoy one of the quaintest and most lovely cities in all of California: Santa Barbara. Plan to be back in SLO one evening to enjoy the Sunset Drive-In Theater. Rent a mountain bike to explore Poly Canyon or Montaña de Oro or a road bike to get out into the rolling hills of the Central Coast.

Watching a sunset at Morro Strand is the perfect way to finish any day

Precautions

While outdoors in the Central Coast, there are two things that you will likely encounter and should know how to spot and avoid: poison oak and ticks.

Poison oak is abundant throughout the Central Coast in California. This leafy green vine or shrub grows along many trails. The easiest way to identify this plant is that the leaves almost always grow in threes. See in the photo how each stem has three leaves? Remember the saying: "Leaves of three? Let it be!" Peak flowering occurs in spring from March to June. The leaves also turn a pretty red. When touched, the spiked wooden twigs and vines — but especially the leaves — cause reactions that vary from nothing to  extreme itching and allergic rashes. As such, long pants are recommended, especially on trails which tend to have less maintenance done. Wash anything that comes in contact with poison oak with soap and water.

Ticks are nasty little buggers that like to wait on the tips of grass and shrubs for their prey to walk by. They are usually no bigger than the tip of a pencil or the length of a fingernail. To avoid, stay on trails and wear long pants. They typically gravitate to the crevices of our bodies: crotch, armpits, behind the ears, scalp. Make it a habit to look yourself over after you hike. Depending on who you're hiking with, offer to help check them over too. If bit, use fine tweezers and remove as soon as possible. Pull out close to the head, straight and steady with  even pressure so you don't break the tick apart. Save the tick for identification. Once out, wash the area with rubbing alcohol or soap and water. If you get flu-like symptoms and a painless rash that grows in size, see a doctor immediately.

SLO City Tour and Cerro San Luis
Urban Hiking with a Bonus Peak

What to Bring: hat, sunscreen, water, picnic items (blanket, plates, cheese, knife, napkins, and a backpack for your booty)
When to Go: Anytime
Duration/Distance: 1–10 miles

Directions to Start: Begin downtown
Want to pack in the best of the city of SLO in one day? This is the adventure for you. This will give you a great taste of what SLO has to offer and leave you yearning for more.

Railroad District (Optional)
Start with an energy-filled breakfast over in the Railroad District, an apt starting point since the railroad is responsible for SLO's growth. Perhaps walk up the stairs for the railroad bridge overpass known as the Jennifer Street Bridge and check out the *killer views*. Come down and take a look at the bronze statue that pays homage to the railway workers. If you want to learn more about the entire area and have plenty of time on your hands, the San Luis Obispo Historical Society has a set of videos online explaining how much of the surrounding area came to be, along with a good walking tour: https://www.youtube.com/user/historycenterslo0638/playlists

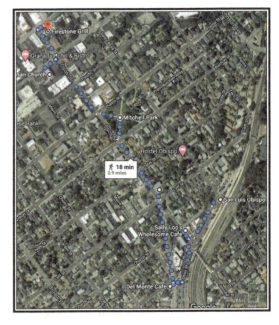

If you're the natural/organic type, you'll love the great breakfast options, coffee and baked goods at Sally Loo's. If you prefer a greasy spoon, head around the corner to Del Monte Café or go to Louisa's Place downtown. If a breakfast burrito is calling to you, Gus's are top-notch. After you eat "brekkie," walk along Osos Street to see part of the pretty residential area downtown. Walk past Mitchell Park, which has a decent children's play area but also tends to have a handful of homeless people hanging about due to the nearby church doubling as a soup kitchen. If you want a very quick detour, go left on Marsh and walk a few doors down to Morro Street. At the corner of Marsh and Morro, take a look at the cool old First Presbyterian Church that was built in 1905 with granite from Bishop Peak. Go back up to Osos Street and continue in the direction you were going toward the main part of town, Downtown SLO.

Sally Loo's

Train Station with Cerro San Luis and Bishop Peak

Downtown SLO

This charming area is the heart of San Luis Obispo and is meant for walking. You'll find many locally run shops with unique items. The main drag is Higuera ("high-gear-ah"). Downtown is basically from Marsh Street to Palm Street and Johnson Street to Nipomo Street with several great businesses just outside that range. I guarantee that part of what is listed below will be different when you read this. Downtown SLO has been changing nonstop and places seem to come and go with more regularity than anyone would like. That means there are always new places to check out, but also that business may not be there for long. I've tried to list places that have been around a while, which means there are plenty left to explore, so don't limit yourself to what I describe.

SLO City Tour and Cerro San Luis

Starting from the corner of Osos Street and Higuera Street in front of Firestone Grill (which is loved by locals for its tri-tip sandos), walk down Higuera Street to see the heart of downtown. Take a left on Morro Street and you'll see the Hotel Granada, which is a great place for dinner or a cocktail; Black Sheep, a great bar that also has many different varieties of mac and cheese; and Eureka Burger, which has the best burgers in town — and yet I even more highly recommend their fried chicken sando. You can thank me later.

Scout's Garden Street location

Go back to Higuera Street and down towards Garden Street stopping off at two terrific spots for unique gifts; Len Collective and Hands Gallery. Contining south, go left on Garden Street to see one of the cutest, most happening areas of downtown. Grab some coffee at either Linneas or Scout. Linneas has our hearts because of their rosemary shortbread cookies and their cute back outdoor space, and Scout pours the best-quality coffee and has THE BEST scones in town plus the morning bun is a game changer. Across from Scout are several shops, all worth visiting.

Back on Higuera, continue left (heading down). Gross yourself out at Bubblegum Alley, then stop at Blast 825 to experience a whole new way of drinking beer and wine. With more than thirty local varieties on tap, get a wristband and serve yourself a "taste" of many types in the search for your favorite.

Fun art and shops in The Mission Mall on Higuera

Go left on Broad for Libertine Brewing Company, which specializes in sour beers. Or go right for Sidecar, which has the best cocktails in town. Keep this in mind for the evening. The cocktails are pricey, but their mixologists are on par with anything you'd expect from the fanciest bars in the fanciest cities.

Back on Higuera, head into the candy store Rocket Fizz, which is worth a look even if you don't want candy. The nostalgia of seeing all your old favorites will bring back pleasant childhood memories. Across the street you'll notice Flour House, where you can enjoy what I consider the best pizza in town. The last stop on this side of the street is Kreuzberg, a great café with really solid food and a good space to do some work.

Cross to the other side of Higuera and take a look at Old San Luis BBQ. This is some seriously delicious barbecue and my go-to for a quick, easy picnic in the plaza. Put this on your mental list of options. Farther down you'll come to Creamery Marketplace, which was a working creamery built in 1906 that operated until 1974.

It was completely redone recently, and now houses some great spots: a coffee shop; bakery; a pleasant place to grab a wine/beer; Mama's Meatball, which is a good option for Italian; Goshi's, which is the best sushi in town; and Nite Creamery Slo, a nitro ice cream spot that regularly has a long line. Fronting Higuera is Mistura, a Peruvian restaurant that offers some of the most interesting fare in the area. Next door is Downward Dog Yoga, widely regarded as the best yoga studio in SLO. If you continue down the street, you'll get to the beginning of the Madonna Mountain hike. We'll get back to that, but first, look back up the street and think about how far you've come. Nearly six blocks, right? That entire stretch of downtown is closed off every Thursday night for the SLO Farmers' Market, which is one of the best farmers' markets in a state known for great farmers' markets. It is a must-do if you happen to be in town on a Thursday night.

Retrace your steps up Higuera and walk through the Creamery past Goshi's in the back, come out the other side to Ciopinot, which offers fantastic seafood. Their signature cioppino dish is remarkable. Go left on Nipomo street and on the right is the Children's Museum. If you have young kids in tow, this is a great way to kill a few hours while they get their wiggles out. If you don't have kids, you might want to stop in at the SLO Museum of Art, which has a good collection of modern art, and the entrance price is right: free.

Now you have a decision to make: Picnic, or lunch at a restaurant? As you've seen, there is no shortage of great restaurants, but if the weather is right, you can't beat a picnic in the town square in the grass next to the Mission. If you're a meat eater, I'd grab a pit plate at Old San Luis BBQ. If you are a vegetarian, you'll have a good option up ahead at Bliss Cafe. If you want to be outside but want to be served, I highly recommend Luna Red, which is just next to the Mission on top of the creek.

Head across the street from Ciopinot to find the walking path that runs next to the San Luis Creek. Take the path along the creek and eventually go up and over a street. Head up the steps and you'll be right in front of Mission San Luis Obispo de Tolosa. If you grabbed BBQ, find a nice spot in the grass to enjoy a picnic. If you want vegetarian, take the bridge over the river and enter the back of Bliss Cafe. Try to coincide your picnic with the turn of the hour since the bells at the Mission go crazy every hour on the hour.

Mission San Luis Obispo de Tolosa

The Mission San Luis Obispo de Tolosa, or, "The Mission," as the locals call it, was founded in 1772 by Father Junípero Serra and named after Saint Louis, Bishop of Toulouse. Back then, the area was teeming with bears, and the Chumash people lived peacefully in the area. The Mission is still used today and opens its doors to the public. Visiting hours are 9 a.m. to 5 p.m. in the summer and 9 a.m. to 4 p.m. the rest of the year. Most days a docent-led tour begins at 1:15 p.m. at the Mission Plaza doors in front of the gift shop (2 p.m. on Sundays). Kids love the "bear fountain" which doesn't quite capture the ferociousness of the Grizzly Bears which used roam this region. Try to be in the plaza at the top of the hour to hear the bells ring.

Cerro San Luis (Madonna Mountain)

Now that you're fed and recharged, it's time to step it up a notch. Literally. Let's go conquer Cerro San Luis, aka Madonna Mountain, aka the mountain behind town with the big 'M' on it. The 'M' actually stands for Mission Prep, the school downtown by the Mission. This hike is also featured in adventure #6, The Tri-Tip Challenge. Fill your water bottle at the drinking fountain in the plaza or at Bliss Cafe, then head south (down) Higuera Street to get to the trailhead. You'll pass the Creamery, a thrift shop, and come to the on-ramp to the 101. Cross under the bridge, which leads you directly to the parking area and trailhead for Madonna

Mountain. Why is this called Madonna Mountain? Because the land is still owned by the Madonna family (one of the founding families of San Luis Obispo), it confusingly has the aforementioned 'M' on the mountain, and, as you head to the trailhead, you look left and see the Madonna Inn. And yet, many people in town get all kinds of bent out of shape when it's called Madonna Mountain. Sorry folks, but if it walks like a duck, has an 'M' on it like a duck, and is owned by the duck, then you just can't argue with the duck.

The start to the popular Cerro San Luis

The trail is wide, really straightforward, and very popular. The view from the top is remarkable and allows you to look down on the entire area you've just explored. Can you make out the Mission? What about other landmarks like San Luis Obispo High School, the tower on top of High School Hill, Cal Poly, the Men's Colony, Morro Rock, Bishop Peak, the 101, and the coastline from Pismo down to Oceano? Take a few deep breaths and enjoy.

SLO City Tour and Cerro San Luis

The view west from Cerro San Luis

Heading back down to the beginning of the trailhead, might you be in the mood for a little dessert? If so, tack on the extra mile to walk to the Madonna Inn to visit what is easily one of the most unique hotels and hotel bathrooms you've ever seen. Do you really want to answer, "I was too tired" when people ask, "Have you seen the bathroom at the Madonna?" Heck no! While I usually set the **EPIC** bar higher, this extra side trip will take this adventure to an entire new level. Once you're at the Madonna, check out the restaurant, the downstairs gift shop, the "hidden" upstairs gift shops (most people don't know about upstairs), and yes, the bathrooms! Then make your way to the café and drool over the cakes. If you thought the hotel was over-the-top eccentric, wait until you see the cakes! They have many types where you can buy a slice. Find

Cake from The Madonna Inn

your favorite and share a piece with a friend or three. If you want an entire cake, however, you better call days ahead — or no cake for you! Because chances are they will not have any sitting around. Their cakes sell like hotcakes. Or something like that. On the way out, get a selfie in the extravagant dining room or in front of the giant fireplace.

Head back up the walking path toward the walking trail, look at the grounds of the Madonna and the hills behind. Is this a beautiful place or what??? Thank you, City of SLO for keeping the natural beauty intact!

Downtown SLO continued

Heading back downtown, head up Higuera, this time on the left (west) side of the road. Stop in at Tom's Toys for two floors of fun. In the event you didn't do the optional side trip to the Madonna Inn, you can make your way up to Doc Burnstein's for some of the best ice cream in town at the coolest ice cream place. To be fair, a few new ice cream spots are giving the Doc a run for his money, including McConnell's Fine Ice Cream on Monterey. Afterward, head back to the corner north of the Mission and walk up Monterey Street. There are a lot of great shops along this stretch, including EcoBambino, which has wonderful gifts for any babies in your life. We always find great used and vintage books at Pegasus Books. If you like music or music memorabilia, Boo Boo Records is a must. A little farther up, you'll find

Music time at BooBoo Records

the SLO Visitors Center, which has a lot of great local information, many nice local souvenirs, and is one of the best places in town to buy high-quality T-shirts.

You are about to enter the SLO Chinese District. But don't get too excited, because as far I can tell, the noodle house Mee Heng Low is the only Chinese establishment that still remains. (Or lo meins, am I right?) But hey, at least we have a Chinese District! Next door is the Palm Theater, which is an outstanding theater for three reasons: 1) They show highly-rated indie films that are not in wide distribution. 2) Tickets are reasonably priced. 3) Popcorn is only $2!!! If you are more of the blockbuster type, Downtown Centre Cinemas is a few blocks over by the Barnes & Noble. Farther up the street is Koberl At Blue, a really cool, dignified building that is nice for a meal or drink. Walk a little farther and you'll come to the Fremont Theater, which usually has some decent bands playing.

If you walk a few blocks up, there are several notable stops: Fiield Day Coffee which is quickly becoming a local favorite;

The Palm & Mee Heng Low

Pipsticks, an adorable sticker shop; Central Coast Brewing, one of the oldest and best craft breweries in town; and Splash Café, which offers some delicious bread bowl clam chowder. If you are a hot dog aficionado and have always wondered how to make them taste even more delicious yet worse for your health, stop in at Frank's Famous Dogs and get yourself a bacon-wrapped hot dog.

You have almost seen it all, but not quite. There are multiple breweries in town, including Central Coast Brewing's second location on south Higuera. Another good option is The Libertine on Broad Street which specializes in sours but has lots of rotating taps. If you want to drive a few minutes, you can check out both Liquid Gravity Brewing and SLO Brew Rock out by the airport.

Central Coast Brewing on south Higuera

SLO City Tour and Cerro San Luis

If your feet are hating you, jump in the car and drive about two miles down Broad Street to Happy Feet for a great one-hour foot massage for less than $40, or check the times for a movie. If you want a really memorable movie experience, get some great food to go and head to the Sunset Drive-in Theater. There are not many drive-in theaters left anymore and the Sunset makes you wonder why. For $9 per adult and $6 per child, you get a double feature, you can bring your own food, and they have concessions available. Bring a blanket and get cozy.

For a nightcap, there are many great options and I highly recommend you barhop to find your favorite. If you don't want to be surrounded by college students, you'll likely enjoy McCarthy's Irish Pub or Black Sheep for a beer. Granada Hotel & Bistro is a bit more upscale and romantic and shh...tucked in next door is Nightcap, a terrific, practically hidden and intimate cocktail bar. Its small, so if there isn't space, try somewhere else and come back. Don't miss stopping in at Sidecar Cocktail Co. — my vote for the best cocktail in town and a great way to end any day.

Grab one of the best cocktails in town at Sidecar

Bishop Peak
The Must-Do SLO Hike

What to Bring: hat, sunscreen, jacket, headlamp, crash pad or climbing gear
When to Go: Always, but best during sunrise or sunset
Duration/Distance: 3.4 miles

Directions to Start: Park on Patricia Drive just past Patricia Court

Before You Start: Drop in at Lassens (closed Sundays) or Sprouts and grab some snacks. Get great coffee on Foothill at either BlackHorse or Scout (morning buns are amazing). If you are the type who exercises so you can eat, the donuts at SloDoCo make every calorie worth the price of working them off.

Of all the mountains in the SLO region, this is the one that you want to "peak." This is by far the most popular hike in the San Luis Obispo area, and for good reason! The terrain is varied, the views are wonderful, the peak is the tallest for many miles, and when you're finished you will feel accomplished. If you are looking for solitude, do this first thing in the morning and/or on weekdays. To make this truly **EPIC**, plan your day to coincide with sunrise or sunset. If sunrise, I highly recommend you bring your morning coffee (in a heat-retaining mug) to enjoy from the top. If sunset, bring a can (no bottles please) of your favorite brew or local wine.

Bishop Peak

Bishop Peak

Park in the residential area off of Patricia Street. Head up the trail and take the path to the left where the dirt trail leaves the paved trail. You'll eventually level off near a holding pond. Cross over past the giant boulders (a great spot for bouldering) and head left as you begin to wrap around from the north side to the south side of Bishop Peak.

As you make your way from the shaded to the sunny side of the mountain, look for the climbing spots in the shade. You will also notice how the foliage and the terrain changes. There is only one way to go now: up. Enjoy some of the best views in town as you ascend. At the top, pull out your snacks and look west to the Pacific and the towns of Cayucos, Morro Bay, and Los Osos. Then turn south and see if you can find Pismo and the Oceano Dunes. Look east and find High School Hill, the location of adventure #3. To the north is the California Men's Colony. As you look at the walls that hold people in, remind yourself how lucky you are to be free and healthy enough to hike this peak! Next to the Men's Colony is a solar project that powers 25 percent of Cal Poly.

California Polytechnic State University
Cal Poly was founded in 1901 and now educates more than 22,000 students each year with more than a quarter enrolled in the College of Engineering. As one of two polytechnic universities within the CSU system, Cal Poly is one of the best schools for agriculture, engineering, landscape architecture, and, perhaps more importantly, was named a Top 10 university for students who want to catch waves while getting a degree by Surfer Magazine in 2018. The students at Cal Poly boast the highest average SAT and ACT scores of any of the 23 California State Universities (CSUs) and the school ranks highest of the CSUs. Which came first: smart people choosing SLO and attending Cal Poly, or Cal Poly only accepting smart people?

Retrace your steps to the open field with the boulders. If you are like most people, you will head back to where you parked and head home. But you are not like most people — you were just getting warmed up! It's time to stretch your legs on the Felsman Loop Trail.

Felsman Loop Trail
This pleasant and easy to follow loop adds 2 miles of extra trail and 570 feet of elevation change along undulating hills and windswept ridges perfect for trail running or hiking and makes for a real muscle burner. Once done, head home with your head high, for you have conquered the biggest and baddest of SLO's seven sisters (there are actually nine Morros in the chain of peaks in this region but you can only access seven of them). Or perhaps make your way over to Milestone Tavern to bask in the glory of your achievement by enjoying a tasty, cold beverage.

Bishop Peak towering over west SLO

High School Hill (Bowden Ranch) and Reservoir Canyon

Great Views, Hard Workout, and No Crowds

What to Bring: hat, sunscreen, water, lunch, snacks, water shoes
When to Go: Anytime
Duration/Distance: 4 miles with optional 5–10 mile extension

Directions to Start: Take Johnson to Lizzy, head uphill, stay left after you pass the adult school. Park near the top of the street. Look for the sign for the trailhead and don't park in the area that clearly states its off limits.

Looking to get in a calf burner of a hike? This is the trail for you. With almost 1,500 feet of elevation gain in just over 1.5 miles, you will feel the burn. Many people complain about this trail because it is so steep, but I find it to be a great place to get a quick, hard workout both up and downhill, especially when prepping for big hikes elsewhere. Prior to a big hiking trip with our young daughters, my wife and I carried our small kids up this hill multiple times a week and then had no problem hiking in the Canadian Rockies (must-do for any hiking enthusiasts!). There is almost no shade anywhere on this hike, so do it early or late, or wear a lot of sunscreen and a hat and bring plenty of water.

High School Hill (Bowden Ranch) and Reservoir Canyon

High School Hill (Bowden Ranch) and Reservoir Canyon

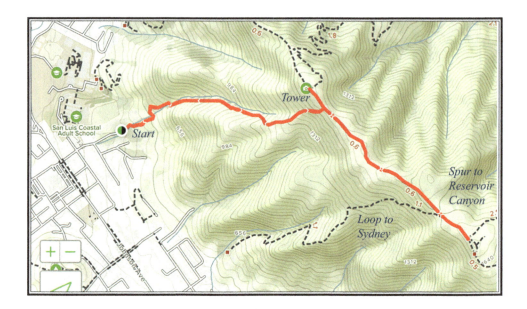

You start on Bowden Ranch Trail with a somewhat gradual ascent through trees and a grove of prickly pear cactus. Within five minutes you will have a great view to the west and a lovely spot to watch the sunset. After you cross over the small seasonal stream, you begin the real hike, which is up, up, up. Believe it or not, the descent is actually harder since you need to carefully place each foot… or you'll be on your rump in no time.

Steep hike up High School Hill

Once at the top, you will have *killer views* in all directions. On a clear day, you will be able to see the Oceano Dunes, Edna Valley, Avila Beach, Morro Bay, and most of the Morros (mountains) from San Luis Obispo to the sea. Head left to the tower to get a nice place to sit, stretch, or meditate. Head right for a nice flat walk along the top of the mountain. Sunsets are glorious from the top, but with the new city ordinance in place that declares trails officially closed one hour after sunset, be sure to give yourself enough time to descend.

High School Hill (Bowden Ranch) and Reservoir Canyon

Sun setting between Cerro San Luis and Bishop Peak

From the tower, you have three options: 1) Return the way you came, 2) Make it a loop by heading along the top of the mountain for about a mile, go right and follow the fire trail down (eventually turns into Sydney Street), or 3) Turn this hike into an adventure by combining this hike with the one down via Reservoir Canyon, which puts you on the opposite side of the mountain from where you started.

Do option 2 for a less steep descent and a slightly longer hike. Using the fire trail includes walking past signs labeled "private property" and going over three cattle fences. Locals have been doing this for years, but please be respectful so all can continue to enjoy using this path.

One of the cattle fences on the Sydney St trail

High School Hill (Bowden Ranch) and Reservoir Canyon

If you take this loop, the trail will lead directly to the top of Sydney Street, and you'll then need to circle back via Johnson to get back to your car.

If you spring for option 3's Reservoir Canyon Trail, you are an adventure seeker and in great shape! This option adds 4.9 miles and 1,282 feet of elevation gain.

From the tower, walk past the turnoff for the fire trail in option 2 and go an extra few hundred feet to the marked trail that drops down to the left, which is the back side of High School Hill. This is Reservoir Canyon Trail. Your few miles of descent will include passing a tree swing and eventually dropping down to the creek. Watch out for the poison oak by the creek that is seemingly always prevalent there. Follow the creek until you get to the waterfall. Hot? Time to let the cool water rush over your head. Nothing beats a quick cool-off from a waterfall. What's under the falls? You'll have to see for yourself. About 100 feet past the falls is Reservoir Canyon Road.

Watch closely on the ridge for the spur to Reservoir Canyon

From the road, you can do one of two things:

1) If you're tired, head toward Highway 101 and walk down the shoulder until you cross over a small bridge that cuts into my favorite neighborhood in town on San Luis Drive. Follow San Luis Drive past the high school and cut up the steep hill just at the end of the high school parking lot. After you pass the front of the school, stay on the driveway on the left and you'll end up on Lizzy Street, turn uphill to retrieve your car.
2) Go back up and over the mountain to where you started. This option gives you more than 3,000 feet of elevation gain!

Pat yourself on the back for a solid adventure completed. Now go out and eat anything you want ... you deserve it!

Southwest Bike Loop to Avila
Easy to Moderate Ride with Ocean Reward

What to Bring: helmet, sunscreen, water, a good book, towel, bike lock
When to Go: Anytime
Duration/Distance: 10 miles each way with optional 3-mile extension

Directions to Start: Anywhere in SLO

One of the best bike rides in the area is from downtown SLO to Avila Beach. Most regular cyclists would consider it easy, but people who don't ride very often would call it moderate. There are bike lanes for the entire duration of the ride, so you can drop your defensive riding a bit and spend more time enjoying the varied views. After starting in downtown SLO — perhaps at the Cambria Bicycle Outfitter on Monterey with your rental bike — head down Higuera Street and follow it past Los Osos Valley Road, past the Octagon Barn, and continue as far south as it goes, until, eventually, you ride under a bridge for Highway 101, and South Higuera Street turns into Ontario Road.

If you're interested in a hike, there is a nice 3.2-mile loop at Johnson Ranch here.

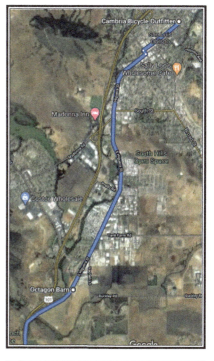

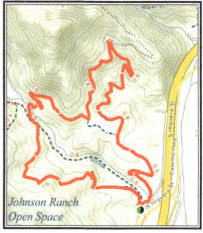

Johnson Ranch

Lock your bike at the trailhead. This relatively easy loop trail takes you through meandering hillsides and is a local favorite.

Once back to the trailhead, hop on your bike as you run parallel to Highway 101 going south.

Ride to Avila continued

At San Luis Bay Drive, you have a decision: You can go right and follow the road toward Avila or you can go straight. I recommend you head straight and come back on San Luis Bay Drive. Going straight a few more minutes on Ontario, you will see a parking lot to your left and the beginning of the Bob Jones Trail to your right. Take the Bob Jones Trail.

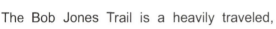

The Bob Jones Trail is a heavily traveled, paved path from Ontario Road that takes you all the way down to the ocean. You will encounter lots of kids wobbling as they work to balance on their bikes. Take your time and enjoy as you make your way down through the Avila Beach Golf Resort and over the bridge, and eventually end at a stoplight for Avila Beach Drive, the main road to and from Avila. Here you can ride directly into Avila and hang out at the beach or continue on the road.

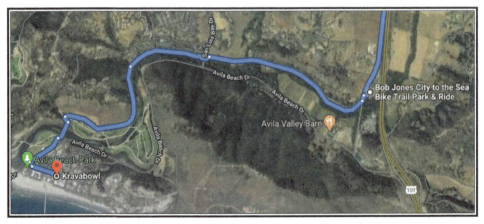

Southwest Bike Loop to Avila

If it's early in the morning, do yourself a favor and head over to KravaBowl in the Avila Market on Front Street and get yourself a giant açaí bowl. The line is worth it! Additionally, *the* place for coffee — Kraken — is just a few doors east from KravaBowl, it is also the best place to work in town, and has ocean views to boot!!

If it's lunchtime, you have two great options: 1) Find a good restaurant along the beach walk, or 2) Continue riding and head to the last stop on the road. I recommend you keep going on the road another few miles where it terminates on Port San Luis Pier. Ride past Fat Cats Cafe out onto the pier. You will likely see fishermen and fantastic views across Avila Bay.

If you're craving seafood (or a beer with a view), saunter over to Mersea's Seafood. The fish is so fresh you'll slap it. The views are incredible and the pricing is exceptionally reasonable. It's impossible not to get an amazing view of the ocean in any direction you look. I like sitting right next to the water to watch the sea lions swim and play around below. I know you're on a bike ride now, but come back sometime to catch an unforgettable sunset.

Have a staring contest with one of the neighbors living under Mersea's

EPIC: Does looking at that water make you wish you could glide on it to get a completely different view of Avila? If so, head back over the pier and across the parking lot to Avila Beach Paddlesports and rent a kayak. My favorite thing to do is to head out through the bay and go east along the coast to the beach that appears just near the rocks sheltering the bay. Enjoy what is almost guaranteed to be your own secluded beach. Perhaps take the quick walk up the trail to check out the Port San Luis Lighthouse which offers tours a few days each week (reservations recommended through www.pointsanluislighthouse.org/about). Back in your 'yak, if you are super lucky, you will get scared silly when a whale swims into the bay while making its biannual migration. However, its much more common to see otters and perhaps dolphins.

Sunset from the end of the pier in Avila

After finishing on the water or pier, head back the way you came and ride into Avila. Perhaps find a good spot to kick it on the beach and read, grab some ice cream or a coffee, or just go for a walk along the beach. If it's "beer thirty," Custom House on the main drag overlooking the ocean is a great spot to enjoy a brew. Or you can brown-bag it by heading to the Avila Market to get your favorite local beer to take with you wherever you like. Finally, there is a great little winery downtown called Alapay, which is definitely worth a stop.

The bay in Avila

When you are ready to leave Avila, you will want to start back the way you came on the Bob Jones Trail. About halfway, you have two options: 1) Continue on the

Bob Jones Trail back to Ontario Road and follow the road back north to SLO the way you came, or 2) Go left on San Luis Bay Drive, follow for about 0.5 miles, then head up See Canyon Road to Kelsey See Canyon Vineyards, a beautiful winery set back in the canyon with a creek running by. If you like peacocks, this is a can't miss. Need I say more? Probably, but I'm not going to. You'll need to go see for yourself. After finishing at See Canyon Vineyards, you could continue up See Canyon through some extremely challenging hills with amazing views ... or save that one for another day if and when you are in great biking shape.

Side Trip to See Canyon

Now head back to San Luis Bay Drive, go left onto Ontario Road just before the 101, and take Ontario back the way you came toward SLO. The road will curve right at the Johnson Ranch trailhead (consider a hike if you didn't do so earlier) and turn into South Higuera Street, which will go under the 101 and eventually take you past Trader Joe's and back into town. Any good

Central Coast Brewing on S. Higuera

adventure allows time for celebrating success and this one is no different. Stop in at the incredibly convenient Central Coast Brewing on South Higuera to have your victory drink.

Southwest Bike Loop to Avila

View from Port San Luis Pier at sunset with moon sparkling on water

Southeast Bike Loop: SLO – Arroyo Grande – Pismo Beach – SLO

5

Rolling Hills, Ocean Views, Two Great Towns, Wine Country, and Five Breweries

What to Bring: hat, sunscreen, water, running shoes, snacks, bike lock
When to Go: Anytime, Oct–Feb for monarch butterflies
Duration/Distance: 33 miles, with optional 2–5 mile run and two walking tours

Directions to Start: Begin at the SLO Train Station or next door at Sally Loo's

This is a gorgeous and varied ride that quickly gets you out of town and into the rolling hills outside of SLO. If you're a wine lover or beer drinker, you will have countless reasons to "take a break." Start with an energy smoothie or a breakfast at either Seeds or Sally Loo's. Cross over the tracks at the train station bridge and follow the bike trail to Orcutt Road. Go left (east) on Orcutt then right at the top of the hill where Orcutt and Johnson intersect. Go left on Tank Farm Road as you travel east out of town. You will 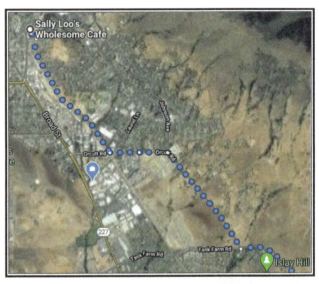 soon pass Baileyana and Tangent wineries and later Chamisal, all of which make for very nice detours.

Go right (south) on Tiffany Ranch Road and left (southeast) on Corbett Canyon Road. Follow Corbett Canyon Road as it turns into Branch Street as you ride into quaint downtown Arroyo Grande. You have now ridden almost 14 miles.

Arroyo Grande

Now you get to check out downtown Arroyo Grande ("AG" is what the locals call it). I like to walk down Branch Street, stop in at a few antique shops, grab a beer at Rooster Creek Tavern, and either grab a slice of pizza at Klondike Pizza (where the floors are covered with peanuts) or some ice cream at the original and very fun Doc Burnstein's. Want more

cuteness? You're in luck! Cross over Short Street, go over the hanging bridge through Centennial Park, and continue over to Heritage Square Park. If you're there on a Sunday in the summer, there's likely an old-timey band playing and folks getting down. Go ahead and join in.

Southeast Bike Loop: SLO – Arroyo Grande – Pismo Beach – SLO

The Hanging Bridge in Arroyo Grande

Now, make your way back to your bike. You can call it a day and ride back the way you came to SLO, or you can start back the way you came but take the 227 through Edna to  get back to SLO or continue on the loop through Pismo.

To continue the loop, head west on Grand Avenue to cruise through the main drag of AG. You will quickly pass over Highway 101. Shortly thereafter, on the right, you will pass Ember Restaurant, many people's pick for the best restaurant in SLO County. A few doors down is Figueroa Mountain Brewing, which is the best brewery in AG. As you pass 3rd Street, The Spoon Trade is on the right, and for my money, is right up there with Ember for some of the best food in the

Southeast Bike Loop: SLO – Arroyo Grande – Pismo Beach – SLO

county. At Highway 1, go right. A quarter-mile up the highway is the Monarch Butterfly Grove on your left.

Monarch Butterfly Grove

If it's late October through late February, stop to see the thousands of monarch butterflies that flock to Pismo Beach every year. There are multiple trails from the monarch grove to the beach, so feel free to take any you want.

Pismo Beach

Continuing northwest on Highway 1, you will reach downtown Pismo Beach. Head left on Pomeroy Avenue and follow it down to the parking lot. Perhaps park your bike and head out to the pier. Of course, you can hang out in Pismo and do any number of great activities. See adventure #26 for more on Pismo.

EPIC: As if this trip isn't **EPIC** enough, I strongly encourage you to add in a run/walk I really love by going down to the beach under the pier and running north along the beach to where the cliffs hit the sea. This round trip on the beach is only a few miles but is a gorgeous and varied stretch.

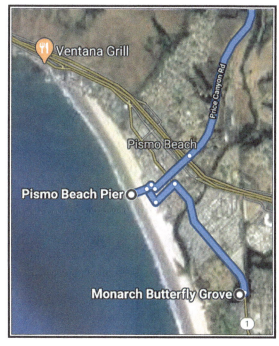

Price Canyon

After the pier, hop back on your bike and head up Hinds Avenue as it becomes Price Canyon Road. This stretch is best completed outside of rush hour, as it gets pretty busy around 4 p.m. to 6 p.m. during weekdays. Price Canyon eventually ends at Highway 227. You are now (momentarily) in Edna Valley. Go left on 227 and perhaps stop in Old Edna for a wine tasting at the Sextant tasting room or else follow 227 for a mile.

Re-entering SLO

Are you feeling more like beer and/or getting back home, or wine and/or less traffic? If the former, stay on 227 as it turns to Broad Street and passes Tolosa Vineyard, the airport, SLO Brew Rock, Liquid Gravity, Broad Street Public House, and eventually right to the Libertine downtown.

If you don't like the extra traffic on 227, go right on Biddle Creek Road where you will pass Biddle Ranch Vineyard, Edna Valley Vineyard, and the Saucelito Canyon Tasting Room. Once you hit Orcutt, go left. You now follow Orcutt back to the bike path and

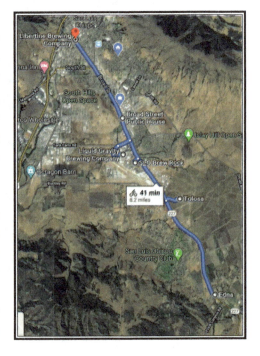

Southeast Bike Loop: SLO – Arroyo Grande – Pismo Beach – SLO

follow the bike path into town. There is great stop along the bike path at Bang The Drum Brewery where you can get solid beers and they have a limited menu of food including meat pasty's served up in a lush, inviting indoor/outdoor setting. This is a great way to recharge after your long ride.

If you did the full loop, you have just completed 33 miles of an **EPIC** biking tour of the towns Arroyo Grande and Pismo Beach and hopefully enjoyed a brewery or winery along the way. Not a bad way to spend day!

Biddle Ranch Vineyard is one of many great wineries along your route

Tri-Tip Challenge
Peak SLO's Most Iconic Hikes in a Single Day

What to Bring: hat, great walking/hiking shoes, sunscreen, water, snacks
When to Go: Anytime
Duration/Distance: 10+ miles

Directions to Start: Bishop Peak parking lot on Foothill Drive

SLO County is known for its tri-tip, which is a cut of meat that is thinly sliced, marinated, and delicious. So what could be more **EPIC** than conquering three of the top peaks in the region in one day, then celebrating your feat by eating — you guessed it — tri-tip? This adventure is not for the faint of heart, the weak of heart, or for anyone with a weak, faint heart. This adventure will get your heart pounding, your calves burning, and your sweat glands in overdrive.

Bishop Peak

You can do this adventure in any order, but my preferred method is to start with Bishop first thing in the morning to avoid the crowds. Extra credit if you get up at dawn to watch the sunrise. See adventure #2 for options at Bishop and directions.

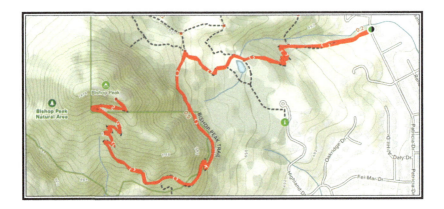

Tri-Tip Challenge

Photos of Cerro San Luis & Bishop as seen from Terrace Hill

Cerro San Luis

After Bishop, drive or bike to the trailhead for Cerro San Luis, aka Madonna Mountain (adventure #1), perhaps stopping for a pit plate at Old San Luis BBQ before or after. I like to take my pit plate down to the creek behind Old San Luis BBQ and unleash the dogs (and by dogs, I mean my hot little toes) for some much-needed cooling off in the creek.

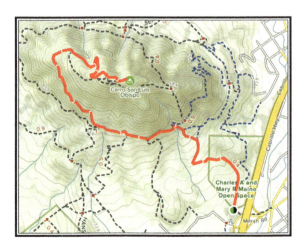

Bowden Ranch Trail (High School Hill)

Once you've summited your second peak, make your way over to Bowden Ranch Trail, aka Fireman's Hill, aka High School Hill (adventure #3), and finish the day with this calf-burner while enjoying a gorgeous sunset.

Finished? You are a beast! Now go get that tri-tip. Head over to Firestone Grill on Higuera and treat yourself to a great sandwich or large plate. You earned it.

Nothing about this day is easy; everything about it is **EPIC**!

Tri-Tip Challenge

Bonus! If the Tri-Tip Challenge is too easy for you or you are working your way up to killer shape, consider kicking it up a notch from the Tri-Tip Challenge to…

Morro Mania

Morro Mania is when you do all five publicly accessible Morros (mountains) in the same day. In total, you'll get in 13 miles and more than 3,500 feet of elevation gain. You'll drop High School Hill from your day but add some of the Morro Bay peaks and end your adventure (on a clear day) with an ocean sunset overlooking all of Morro Bay. Pick a day in late fall or early spring (or a cooler summer day), so you'll have more daylight, since you're going to need the extra hours. Thanks to the local Santa Lucia chapter of the Sierra Club, which is where I first heard about this calf-burning adventure.

You can go in any order you prefer, but here is a proposed itinerary:

7:30 a.m. – Islay Hill – 2 miles and 500 feet of elevation gain. From the Orcutt intersection, take Spanish Oaks to Sweetbay Lane, go left. Park in cul-de-sac.

9 a.m. – Cerro San Luis – 4 miles and 1,100 feet of elevation gain. Park at Marsh Street just before the Highway 101 on-ramp. Grab a lunch to go or bring your picnic.

12 p.m. – Bishop Peak – 3.5 miles, 950 feet of elevation gain. Park at the trailhead on Patricia Drive. Picnic at top.

3:30 p.m. – Cerro Cabrillo – 2.5 miles, 800 feet of elevation gain. Park at the easy-to-miss Quarry Trail trailhead on South Bay Boulevard.

6 p.m. – Black Hill – 3 miles, 650 feet of elevation gain. Park in Morro Bay State Park on Main Street in the parking area at the end of the road.

Just when you thought things couldn't get any **EPICer**, you go out and do something like this! If you completed Morro Mania, you are a maniac. I'll apologize in advance for how sore you'll be in the coming days. But you earned every ache and pain, and when those annoyances are long forgotten, you'll still be able to enjoy your memory of crushing five Morros in a day!

Tri-Tip Challenge

Views from the easiest of the 5 Morros: Islay Hill

Mountain Bike West Cuesta Ridge and Down Poly Canyon

Convenience, Climb, and Canyon Make for an EPIC Ride

What to Bring: biking gear, sunscreen, water, walking shoes
When to Go: Anytime
Duration/Distance: 2–3 hours

Directions to Start: Start at San Luis Obispo High School

This is one of the best, most convenient, and popular bike rides you can do starting from SLO. There is nothing particularly technical about this ride; the hardest part is the ascent. If you can ride a bike, you can do this adventure. Prior to setting out, you can do some additional research on the trails here: https://www.mtbproject.com/directory/8012699/san-luis-obispo

In the event you don't have a mountain bike, head to Foothill Cyclery on Foothill Blvd or Cambria Bicycle Outfitter on Monterey Street next to Central Coast Brewing and they'll hook you up with all the gear you need.

There are two main ways to get to the starting point of the ride, which is at the top of "the grade" (this is the hill one takes to leave SLO on Highway 101 north of SLO). Many who ride mountain bikes in SLO will eventually do both, but most prefer riding up and down Poly Canyon versus up Old Stagecoach Road. I recommend Poly Canyon for your first time, but I'll give you directions for both, plus a third, easier option which cuts out the work of the ride up.

Poly Canyon Ascent

From Cambria Bicycle Outfitters, head up Monterey Street and go left on Grand Avenue. Follow Grand into the Cal Poly campus as it turns into Perimeter Road then Village Drive, then Poly Canyon Road. You'll follow Poly Canyon Road for a few miles and will pass the Poly Canyon Design Village aka the Cal Poly Architecture Graveyard on your left (save this fun detour for the descent). Continue along Poly Canyon Road until you can go right on Red Dog. Follow Red Dog through the fun bike obstacle course and ascend Shooters and the Shooters Connector, which is the most popular mountain biking stretch in SLO. Once you do it, you'll see why. This is what mountain biking is all about. As you ascend, keep an eye out for descending mountain bikers. Once you reach the top, you will be on TV Tower Road.

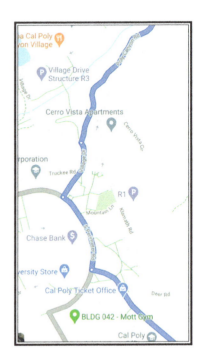

Old Stagecoach Road Ascent

Head north past SLO High School on San Luis Drive. At the end of the street, you'll see a dirt trail that leads to the 101. Ride along the shoulder of the 101 North. Yes, this is sketchy, so be careful! At Old Stagecoach Road, you'll cross over the 101 to the dirt road. Ever played Frogger? This is your chance to do it in real time. Keep in mind that cars are going 70+ mph, so make sure there is a nice, long opening before crossing the road. Get ready for a real leg burner! Riding up the grade on Old Stagecoach Road will put you to the test. At the top, you'll reach TV Tower Road where you'll go left. A longer option which lets you avoid the 101 altogether is to first ascend via Poly Canyon until you get to the railroad tracks then follow the tracks until you get to tunnel. Go right and descend to Old Stagecoach Road then ascend until you get to TV Tower Road.

Mountain Bike West Cuesta Ridge and Down Poly Canyon

The Easy Way Up
For this one, you're going to need a riding partner and a second vehicle. Leave one car at the bike shop and drive one car to the parking lot at the top of the grade, thereby avoiding biking up the grade and along the 101. Park on the west side of the freeway in the parking lot for the West Cuesta Ridge, which is also known as TV Tower Road.

TV Tower Road
If you ascended on Old Stagecoach or drove to the West Cuesta Ridge trailhead, you now ride west along the ridge. The semi-paved road is in rough shape. Check out the glorious views back down toward SLO. When you come to a fork in the road where it turns to dirt, this is the top of Shooters and where the fun begins.

Shooters
No matter which way you ascended, you should now be at the top of the most popular and fun span of dirt in SLO. This spur is called Shooters and gives you everything you might hope for in a ride. Within a few hundred feet of your descent, you will ride past a gate closing the road to automobiles. The road starts out relatively wide and offers glorious views to the valley below. Then it narrows to two single tracks and you will need to choose right or left. The trail on the right is Shooters Trail. This is the one you want. The trail to the left of Shooters is Roller Coaster Trail, which is better for hiking.

Mountain Bike West Cuesta Ridge and Down Poly Canyon

Wind in your face, speed, *killer views* — this is your reward for the work you put in to get out here. You'll bomb down quickly, so enjoy every second. The views of the track ahead are good throughout this whole section. Keep an eye out for a fence where you'll need to walk your bike through. About a mile down Shooters, you'll meet up with Elevator Trail — take this down to Stenner Trail. After about a mile, you'll want to take Poly Canyon Road on your left. This will take you 3.7 miles down to Cal Poly. If you've never done the hike to Poly Canyon Design Village, here's your chance. On this brief side trip, you can check out the unique and interesting efforts of the architecture teams from years past. Which design is your favorite?

Leaning Pine Arboretum

Keep a lookout for people as you get closer to Cal Poly since this road is used by hikers and runners. Next up on your adventure is a highly worthwhile side trip if it's between 8a.m. and 5 p.m. Monday to Friday. While riding down Poly Canyon Road, take the spur on the right to Brizzolara Creek Trail. This dirt trail is easy to miss, so keep an eye out. This little shortcut takes you to Canyon Circle, where you'll go right, continue on to Village Drive, go right on Via Carta, and head to the Leaning Pine Arboretum on your right. This little-known arboretum is a gorgeous spot and makes for a great location to enjoy a book, a picnic, or both!

Hike the Poly P

Head toward campus on Via Carta and go left on Village Drive. Follow the road through campus and past

where it meets up with Poly Canyon Road. It is time for a quick little bonus hike to the Poly P which is a giant P on the side of a hill behind Cal Poly. Go left on Klamath Road and you will quickly come to a huge parking lot. In the middle, nearest the hill, is where you can hop, skip, and jump — or just walk — up to the P. Once you get your selfie at the P, ride down Klamath until you get to Grand Avenue, and go left. Stay on Grand, which will take you under the freeway and back to Monterey Street. At Monterey, go right and head back to your starting point, which is conveniently located across from...

Bread Bowls & Beer
Now that you've worked up a solid appetite, grab yourself a clam chowder bread bowl at Splash Café, then a beer at Central Coast Brewing. Or, if you really want to walk on the wild side, head to Frank's Famous Dogs and get yourself a bacon-wrapped hot dog and a milkshake. This might be the most heart-stopping part of your entire adventure!

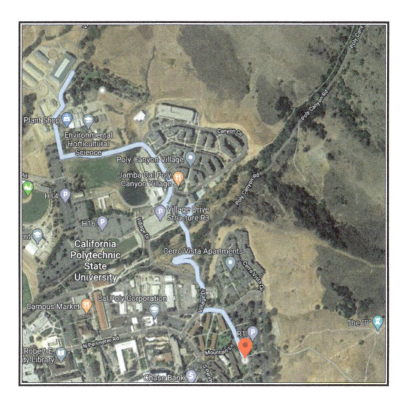

Western Bike Loop to Los Osos and Morro Bay

8

Lovely Ride West of Town Through Rolling Hills with Optional Stops in Los Osos and Morro Bay

What to Bring: sunscreen, sunglasses, windbreaker, extra layer, water, fix a flat tools, bike lock

When to Go: Mornings are best to avoid typical afternoon winds blowing in from the west

Duration/Distance: ~3–5 hours and 27–38 miles

Directions to Start: Downtown SLO on Chorro at the Mission

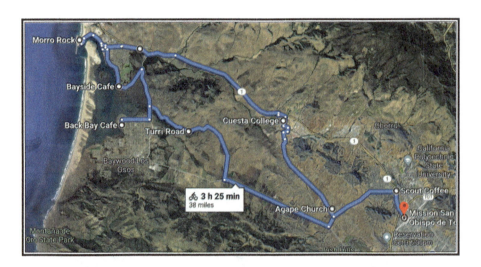

This bike ride west of San Luis Obispo gets you off the main roads and into the gorgeous countryside, with the bonus of optional extensions that take you along the beautiful coast. Many people do this western bike loop in a counterclockwise fashion, starting on Highway 1, going to Morro Bay, then down to Los Osos Valley Road (LOVR) and back. But if riding along highways is as unnerving for you as it is for me, you will likely enjoy the route described below that offers the same distance but minimizes time on busy LOVR and Highway 1 and maximizes time in lovely rolling hills.

Western Bike Loop to Los Osos and Morro Bay

Starting in downtown SLO at Chorro by the Mission, or really anywhere in SLO, make your way west to Foothill Street. Get your caffeine fix at Scout or BlackHorse, or grab an amazing donut at SloDoCo (each location makes for a great meetup spot), then head south on Foothill toward LOVR. You will quickly be out of town and into open space. Look right to see one trailhead for Bishop Peak and look left to spot cattle grazing at Madonna Ranch. Just prior to LOVR, you will pass O'Connor Way — this is the way you will loop back.

Go right (west) on LOVR toward the water. Ride for approximately three miles until you reach Turri Road, then go right. I lived in SLO for more than five years before learning about this gorgeous road, which is lightly traveled and takes you through lovely rolling hills. Take a break at the top of Hinds Summit where someone has thoughtfully added Kevy's Bench.

Continue all the way to South Bay Boulevard. Take a minute to get a selfie with the Los Osos Bear.

At South Bay Boulevard, you have the option of adding more stops to your ride: Los Osos (3.3 miles round trip) and Morro Bay (2.3 miles with another optional addition of Morro Rock for another 3.4 miles).

Turri Road was made for biking

Take a quick break at Hinds Summit and enjoy the sprawling views west

Western Bike Loop to Los Osos and Morro Bay

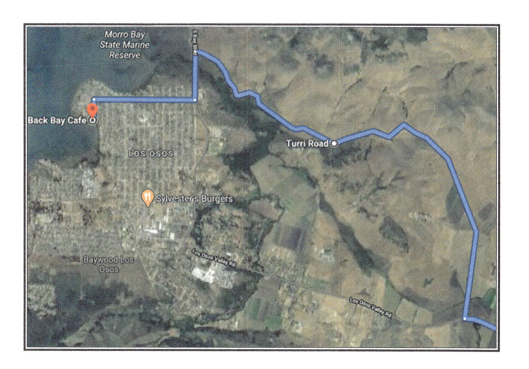

For Los Osos, go left on South Bay Boulevard, then right on San Ysabel. Ride to 2nd Street, then go left. Several good restaurants, including the Back Bay Café, line the street. Take your pick for a snack, or just enjoy the view from next to the Back Bay Café. Head back to South Bay Boulevard and go left.

For Morro Bay, go right on South Bay Boulevard, follow the signs pointing left for Morro Bay State Park, as you turn left you are on Main Street. This will wrap you around Morro Bay State Park and allow you to enter Morro Bay from the south. Just past the campground, you can stop for a bite at the Bayside Café and enjoy the view of the water. From here, you can retrace your route back to South Bay Boulevard or add a little climbing by continuing along Main Street then riding through the golf course by taking a right on Park View, which takes you back toward Bay Boulevard. Or, you are strongly encouraged to extend your ride into downtown Morro Bay and make your way along the waterfront to Morro Rock. If you make it to Morro Rock and you haven't stopped for a bite or a snack yet, I highly recommend grabbing a smoothie or a bite at either Shine Café or Goddess Goods (which is right on your way). Both have wonderful and healthy options. If it's a nice day, you'll want to take your makeshift picnic down by the water to enjoy while watching the sea otters play.

Western Bike Loop to Los Osos and Morro Bay

Sea Otters galore in Morro Bay

In all cases, you will eventually want to get on Quintana Road which runs perpendicular to South Bay Boulevard. Heading east from South Bay Boulevard on Quintana, you'll momentarily parallel Highway 1. Make sure you stop for a moment prior to getting on the highway to enjoy the view of Hollister Peak, which many consider the loveliest of the Morros. Then, pedal on and you'll be on the highway heading back east toward SLO.

Western Bike Loop to Los Osos and Morro Bay

At Cuesta College, you can either continue along Highway 1, which will take you to Foothill, or turn off the highway and take the back way through Cuesta College

and the Camp San Luis Obispo Military Campground back to Foothill. This alternative adds 1.9 miles to your ride but is much more pleasant than Highway 1. There is really only one way to go but it requires many turns as you weave through the complex. Follow Hollister Road to Colusa Avenue, go right on O'Connor Way, go left and follow to Sutter Avenue, quick left and right, and you're back on O'Connor Way. Take this road through extremely beautiful countryside back to Foothill Boulevard.

Go left on Foothill and you'll be back where you started. Great job, don't forget to stretch so you can walk tomorrow! You have earned yourself a refreshment. Stop by Milestone Tavern, where they have dozens of tasty beverages on tap. Or grab an iced mocha at BlackHorse, get something healthy over at Lassens, or make your way downtown for endless options.

Big Sur in a Day

Mystery, Adventure, and Unbelievable Beauty Make for an Unforgettable Day

What to Bring: hat, sunscreen, water, picnic, full tank of gas, beach gear, hiking shoes, warm layers

When to Go: Anytime

Duration/Distance: 6–10 hours

Directions to Start: From SLO, take Highway 1 North

Adventure Agenda	Option 1	Option 2
Breakfast	Big Sur Bakery	At home
Morning adventure	Bluff Trail Loop	Pfeiffer Beach
Lunch/Afternoon	Big Sur Taphouse	Valley View at Pfeiffer Big Sur State Park
Late Afternoon	Andrew Molera Beach Trail	Nepenthe or Deetjen's and Henry Miller Memorial Library
Sunset	Partington Cove Trail, McWay Falls	Sea Lions near Piedras Blancas Light Station
Dinner	Schooners	Sea Chest or Taco Temple

A day trip to Big Sur is unlike any other in this book. Big Sur is a mysterious place — hanging from the cliffs, overlooking the Pacific, covered in redwoods, and typically shrouded in fog most of the day. Before you leave the majesty of the area, you will already be plotting your return. Big Sur offers adventure and sublime beauty.

Big Sur in a Day

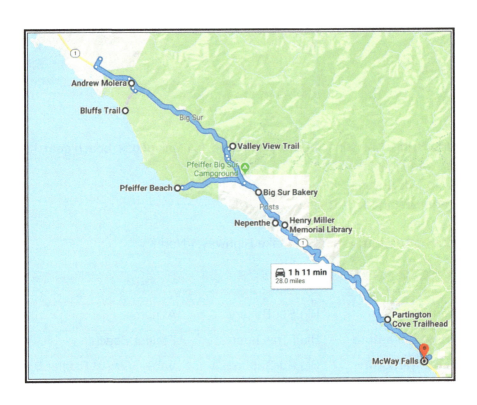

Hare Creek Trail in Limekiln State Park

Big Sur in a Day

In this adventure, you will get to experience some of the top highlights of the area. To get off the beaten path a bit more, you might want to jump ahead and pick some of the options from the subsequent Big Sur North and Big Sur South adventures (#10 and #11). If you go through all three adventures and want even more, check out one of the many books devoted entirely to this magnificent stretch of coast. Big Sur is also a great camping destination and I strongly encourage you to stretch any trip to two days or more, as you will no doubt want to linger as long as time, money, and weather permit. I mention weather because the road to Big Sur, especially south of town, has been closed numerous times due to heavy rain. If you're heading up after a rain, check the forecast and conditions ahead of time — or you will drive all the way to Gorda before you know you need to turn around. Don't ask me how I know this.

The best way to go about a day trip is to leave from SLO via Pacific Coast Highway, make a beeline straight to Big Sur, then use any extra time you have on the way back to make other stops. Prior to heading up, please strongly consider taking Big Sur Pledge.

Big Sur Pledge
I pledge to:

- Share our coastal roads in a safe manner.
- Be mindful of the impact of my actions.
- Protect and respect Big Sur's natural resources, public and private property, residents, employees, and visitors.
- Leave no trace; and not damage or take what is not mine.
- Camp only where allowed.
- Be vigilant and fire safe.
- Be a steward of this precious resource for the enjoyment of all.
- Honor the spirit of Big Sur as it honors me.
- Put the pledge into action.

This pledge was created by Big Sur locals who want to make sure the area retains its beauty and that those who come to experience the area do so respectfully. Hopefully you will incorporate the spirit of this pledge into your Big Sur adventures and extend its principles throughout your journeys elsewhere.

Big Sur Bakery

Just about everyone who goes through Big Sur stops at Big Sur Bakery (opens at 8 a.m.), an institution in the area that makes some of the finest food and definitely the best coffee in the region. Get there outside of peak mealtimes or you'll be standing in a line thirty deep. And yet, even with inflated Big Sur prices and a huge line, it's still worth it! This is a great stop for grabbing baked goods and fresh bread to go. But don't get there too late or all the day's goodies will be  gone. On multiple occasions, the fresh baked bread has been sold out for the day when I've stopped in at 11 a.m.

Pfeiffer Beach

Another spot you need to show up early: Pfeiffer Beach. If it's the weekend during any but the slowest times of year, the latest you could arrive and still hope to get a spot is 10 a.m., or else you'll be turned away. Sunrises and sunsets are particularly wonderful here. Let's assume you hit Big Sur Bakery at 8 a.m., then get to Pfeiffer Beach by 9 a.m., or perhaps you head straight to Pfeiffer Beach for sunrise. You can do a lovely 0.9-mile walk along the beach.

For a spot that is on every Big Sur to-do list, you might be surprised to learn that there is no sign indicating Pfeiffer Beach's whereabouts. Big Sur also has horrible phone service, so you'll want to make sure you have the address in your phone ahead of time or you won't be able to find it on GPS. To get there, go half a mile north of Big Sur Bakery and turn on the sharp left. From the north, go one mile south of the entrance to Pfeiffer Big Sur State Park and take the second right. There are typically attendants just after the turnoff who will make you turn around if the parking lot two miles down the road is full.

Big Sur in a Day

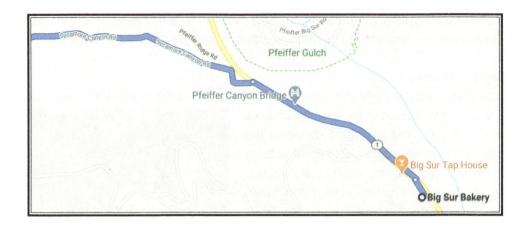

After Pfeiffer Beach, stretch your legs with a hike where you can get into the redwoods, enjoy a waterfall, and see what makes Big Sur so special. Depending on how you're feeling, choose one of the options below:

- Bluff Trail Loop just north of Andrew Molera Beach Trail – 8 miles, moderate. (See detailed info in Big Sur North chapter #10)
- Andrew Molera Beach Trail – 2.3 miles, easy walk.
- Valley View at Pfeiffer Big Sur State Park – 1.8 miles, moderate, best hike to do if you're going to do just one.
- Partington Cove Trail – 0.9 miles, moderate.

Big Sur in a Day

I usually like to start farther north and bite off the harder hike in the morning, then enjoy a picnic lunch, and after that, do an easier hike in the afternoon while traveling south. So, depending on what shape you're in, you'll want to do the Bluff Trail, Andrew Molera Beach Trail, or Valley View first thing. Depending on the time, you'll want to bring a picnic or some snacks since all have great spots for sitting, pondering, and snacking. Three of my favorite things to do!

Heading back through the main part of town, you may want to grab some grub at the Big Sur Taphouse, which feels like a hidden gem. Make sure you check out the back patio, which is huge and perfect for enjoying a cold one.

Walking through redwoods on Valley View Trail

If you're looking for something a bit fancier and don't mind paying $18 for a burger, enjoy an incredible view and a cocktail at Nepenthe. For some people, a drink or a meal here will be the most memorable part of the trip. You've been warned: The place is pricey, so set your expectations accordingly and factor the view into the price of your food and drinks. Would you pay $12 for a burger and $6 for a fireside seat where you can see a *killer sunset* over the Pacific? If yes, then reconsider how you look at that $18 burger and enjoy one of the best views, wash it down with a beer, and enjoy the warming fire. It's totally worth it!

Another great option if you're going upscale is Deetjen's. This intimate little gem is tucked into the redwoods, and, like many spots in Big Sur, if you don't know it's there, you'll fly right past it. This is a great spot if you're looking for a romantic meal or a place to celebrate. You should make a reservation well in advance if you'd like to dine at Deetjen's on the weekend.

Valley View

After eating, stop off for a moment at the Henry Miller Memorial Library, located one mile south of Nepenthe and one mile north of Deetjen's, to pay homage to one of the pioneers of Big Sur. Prior to starting your day, check the schedule for the charming Henry Miller Memorial Library (https://henrymiller.org/), as it routinely has music and arts events, and a stop there with a picnic is quite lovely.

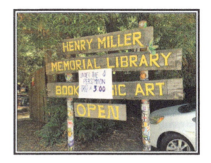

Then head to Partington Cove and make sure you leave time to stop and check out McWay Falls, which is repeatedly rated as one of the most beautiful waterfalls in the U.S. Get some selfies that will make all your friends and family jealous. During high tide, McWay Falls is a tidefall, meaning it empties directly into the ocean. This is one of only two spots in California where that phenomenon occurs. (The other is Alamere Falls in Marin County, which should also be on your list of things to do.) To get to McWay Falls, you have two options: 1) Park on the highway, walk toward the entrance to the park, follow the trail under the road to the viewpoint for the falls, or 2) As you are traveling south, you can park on the shoulder of the highway about 200 feet before the entrance to the park. Walk down the shoulder of the highway and you'll get the same *killer view* of the picturesque waterfall and you'll be above all the tourists below. Choose option 1 if you have the time and option 2 if you've been there before or are in a hurry.

One of the coves at Partington Cove

Big Sur in a Day

On the way back, if you don't have time to do the San Simeon adventure (#12), stop just after Piedras Blancas Light Station to marvel at the sea lions. If you've never seen sea lions up close, this spot will easily be a highlight of your day.

With so much beauty in one day, how do you finish it off? If you haven't done a fancy meal, you might try the seafood at Sea Chest in Cambria. It is cash only and usually has a line, but is worth the wait. We usually end our day at Taco Temple right off Highway 1 in Morro Bay, where

Sea lions skirmish near San Simeon

the portions are so big, every meal is enough for two. Either way, you'll sleep well after this unforgettable day! And no doubt, you will dream of your return.

Sunset from Ragged Point

Big Sur North

Check Out the Northern Part of Big Sur and the "Town" Itself

What to Bring: hat, sunscreen, water, picnic, calves of steel, layers, flashlight

When to Go: Anytime. Longer days in summer. Check on road closures during the rainy season.

Duration/Distance: Day trip with options for many miles of hiking

Directions to Start: From SLO, take Highway 1 to Andrew Molera State Park

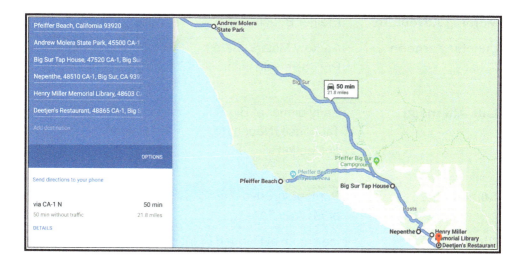

Assuming you've already done some of the best of the Big Sur in a Day Adventure (#9), you've had a taste of this stunning area and you've come back for more. This adventure has some overlap with Big Sur in a Day so you don't miss any of the highlights, but mainly focuses on the northern part of Big Sur down to "town." The town itself is hard to pinpoint since Big Sur is really individual businesses scattered here and there. Heading to the northern part of Big Sur is quite a trek from SLO, so you'll want to get started early and probably go during the non-winter months so you will have more daylight. Alternatively, seriously consider doing an overnight and staying at one of the many campgrounds, cabins, or hotels.

Big Sur North

While you can still backpack and pitch a tent for free, the cheapest camping option these days is $35/night and prices go up quickly from there. Additionally, due to its remoteness, popularity, and inability for large trucks to make deliveries, prices in Big Sur can be astronomical — so consider bringing your own supplies.

You could easily spend many days in northern Big Sur, so depending on how you feel, here is a handy-dandy itinerary builder that allows you to pick how you'd like to spend your day.

Adventure Agenda	Option 1	Option 2
Breakfast	At home	Big Sur Bakery
Morning Adventure	Pfeiffer Beach	Pfeiffer Beach
Lunch/Afternoon	Andrew Molera State Park hike with picnic	Big Sur Taphouse, Henry Miller Memorial Library
Late Afternoon	Early dinner at Big Sur Taphouse, Nepenthe, or Deetjen's	Tanbark Trail and Tin House
Sunset	Partington Cove and/or McWay Falls	Pacific Valley Bluffs
Dinner	Ice cream at Ragged Point and/or grab a drink at Schooners	Wild Coast, Sea Chest, Schooners, or Taco Temple

While Big Sur stretches from Carmel all the way to San Simeon, driving from SLO to Carmel on PCH is three hours each way and has your booty in a seat in a car on a windy road (albeit a majestically beautiful windy road) instead of on an adventure. Hence, I suggest Andrew Molera State Park (2.5 hours from SLO) as the northernmost point for this day trip.

Start your day with a quick "brekkie" at home and take some coffee and morning snacks on the road. Let whoever suffers from motion sickness drive or sit up front. Plan to drive all the way north then begin making your way back south, stopping along the way for adventure. The only exception is if it's the weekend and you haven't been to Pfeiffer Beach yet; in that case, you should try going there as early as possible or parking will be full and you'll be turned away. It's a narrow two-mile road down to the beach and walking in isn't much of an option. 10 a.m. is about the latest you could arrive on a weekend and still hope to get a spot. If you do go, you'll be rewarded with a gorgeous beach with keyhole rocks that make for a photographer's delight. The walk along the beach is just under one mile. Now head to our northernmost destination...

Andrew Molera State Park
Do the Beach, Bluffs, Panorama Ridge, and Creamery Meadow Loop. You'll love this popular 8.2-mile trail. The best way to do the trail is clockwise so that you get the main elevation gain out of the way first, then don't have to work so hard the rest of the way. Definitely have a snack at the peak as a reward. Alternatively, if you have no intention of doing the full loop, go in a counterclockwise direction and turn back whenever it suits you.

Big Creek Bridge

Rock formations below Kirk Creek

Options for Eating

With that big hike behind you, it's time to grab some food. There are three options I highly recommend:

1) For a relaxed environment with great value and the best prices, head to the practically hidden Big Sur Taphouse.
2) For a *killer view* costing $10 and an $8 burger, head to Nepenthe. Actually, I lied: The view is free, but the burger is $18, and at that price, it's the cheapest thing on the menu. But if you take the view into account, it makes the experience easier to stomach. Would you like some ketchup with that pun?
3) Finally, if you're looking for a romantic meal, you can't go wrong with Deetjen's Restaurant. Make sure you call ahead or you will be the creeper longingly looking in the window at others enjoying their romantic meal.

Big Sur North

You've basically just driven through the "town" of Big Sur. Not much to it, right? If you didn't stop at the Henry Miller Memorial Library, it's worth a quick visit for the grounds alone.

From Henry Miller, you have about 2 hours and 15 minutes back to SLO. Depending on your available time, you can head on a big hike to Tanbark Trail and Tin House, do a quick descent to Partington Cove (see below), McWay Falls (detailed in Big Sur in a Day), or any of the activities in the next adventure, Big Sur South.

Tanbark Trail and Tin House

If you like adventures that make you work but are totally worth it, you'll love the Tanbark Trail and Tin House loop! This is a 6.1-mile out-and-back calf burner (7 miles if you make it a loop) with 2,024 feet of elevation and surprises around every corner.

Start at the same parking spot as Partington Cove (see below for parking directions), but head away from the ocean. You will be instantly immersed in a serene setting next to the creek and among redwoods. Enjoy the calm for the first five to ten minutes, eventually you will turn right, from there its up, up, up.

All that hard work has a payoff, as you can expect *killer views* from this trail along the coast and as far as the eye can see. Since the trail is listed as "hard" in any trail description, you'll enjoy more solitude here than at many other Big Sur hikes.

During certain times of year, this trail can get overgrown. This will make it a little less fun, but it's still worth it and very doable. Watch out for poison oak and do a tick check after the hike (which is good practice after doing any hikes in the Central Coast, especially when you brush against foliage).

At the peak of the hike, the remains of the Tin House patio make for a good place to break and eat a snack. For the way back down, you can retrace your steps or take the fire road. If, like me, you're more of a "loop" person, take the fire road down. This will be a little easier on your legs and provides great views, but is also exposed. You'll end up on Highway 1 about a mile south of your car. Cross over the road and walk north along the ocean side so you can see oncoming traffic. This will be the least fun part of the hike. Once you get back to the parking area, keep it going by stitching in the walk to Partington Cove for a completely different experience.

Partington Cove

Like many places in Big Sur, Partington Cove is pretty well hidden. You go around one of a million curves on the road and see a bunch of cars parked and think, "I wonder what's there?" Most drive right on by, but not you, oh loyal reader. In this case, you know that this curve hides a dramatically lovely spot with a lot of variety for relatively little work. Many people consider this short walk one of the highlights of their trip to Big Sur. Here's a photo of the trailhead, which is

Partington Cove Trailhead

basically a road cutting down from PCH. Note the green gate. This trailhead is about five miles south of Deetjen's Restaurant and two miles north of Julia Pfeiffer Burns State Park. With no GPS or cell service, you're going to have to go old school and use your eyes to spot the trailhead.

SLOcals Only **Pro Tip**:

If you go here a bit before sunset, you will have the place mostly to yourself. Bring some layers, as it will be breezy and cool. If you do plan to stay for the sunset, bring a headlamp or make sure your phone is charged so you can use the flashlight.

Head down the gradually descending trail for about fifteen minutes. You will come to a three-way fork. Start with the left fork, then do the middle, then the right. Each is prettier than the last. I would tell you what each offers, but where's the adventure in that?

McWay Falls

Want to round out your **EPIC** day in Big Sur? Assuming you have a bit of sunlight left, here's a quickie for you. Everyone likes a quickie, right? As you head south and near Julia Pfeiffer Burns State Park Vista Point, pull over to park on the ocean side of the road. From the shoulder of the road, you can stand at the edge of the cliffs and see McWay Falls. While many fight for parking in the park and do the full trail, you get the same view but from 20 feet higher, without doing any work. Winning!

Pacific Valley Bluff Trail

As you're driving back, Pacific Valley Bluff Trail usually has beautiful wildflowers along PCH and an easy 1.6-mile roundtrip trail down to the ocean and back. This is a great alternative to Partington Cove if you want a bit of a hike near the water but perhaps don't want as many people around or the steep decline and incline.

Park directly across from the small hill (usually covered in flowers) with a residence behind it. Take a selfie with the gorgeous flowers, then cross over the fence and head toward the ocean. The path is flat, and within moments you'll be on top of rocky cliffs with the Pacific at your feet. If it's nice out or the sun is setting, you may want to sit on the small beach or large rock jutting into the ocean. Oh, the glory of Big Sur!

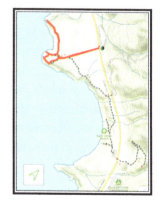

The Beach at Pacific Valley

EPIC Finish

If you're hungry, a good seafood/sushi option is Wild Coast (open until 8 p.m.) at Treebones Resort. (Omakase experience is highly recommended — reservations needed on weekends.) Sweet tooth calling? Stop at the Ragged Point Inn Snack Bar on your way home for ice cream with **EPIC** ocean views. Eat your ice cream while stretching your legs and walking along the bluffs behind the snack bar and watch the sunset or moon reflect off the ocean. There is a very steep trail to a black sand beach below the lookout at Ragged Point. Do it if you're really feeling ambitious but, for my money, sitting up above and enjoying a beer, or ice cream or both is much more fulfilling.

Big Sur North

Grab an ice cream and enjoy Ragged Point views

Other great restaurants farther south that are right on your way include Sea Chest Restaurant in Cambria (cash only, no reservations, open until 9 p.m.). Schooners (open until 9 p.m. on weekdays, 10 p.m. on weekends) in Cayucos is good for bar seafood and great for a drink, especially upstairs at the bar. For a cheaper option, head to Taco Temple in Morro Bay (open until 9 p.m.). No matter which option you pick, you'll be full and happy. Pat yourself on the back for making the most of this amazing day.

Big Sur South

More Great Things to Do in S. Big Sur Not Covered in Big Sur in a Day Adventure

What to Bring: hat, sunscreen, water, picnic, layers, flashlight, water filter
When to Go: Best when the days are long (non-winter months)
Duration/Distance: Daytrip with ~3 hours driving and more than 30 miles of potential exploring

Directions to Start: Take Highway 1 up the coast past San Simeon

The Big Sur South adventure has a little overlap with the Big Sur in a Day adventure, but gives much more detail on all the things you can do in the southern part of the area. The northern boundary of this adventure is just past Gorda at Sand Dollar Beach.

Adventure Agenda	Option 1	Option 2
Breakfast	The Spot in Cambria	At home
Morning adventure	Easy – Redwood Gulch	Moderate - Cruickshank Trail
Lunch/Afternoon	Sand Dollar Beach	Sand Dollar Beach
Late Afternoon	Willow Creek Picnic Area	Jade Cove, Redwood Gulch
Sunset	Partington Cove and/or McWay Falls	Partington Cove and/or McWay Falls
Dinner/Dessert	Ice Cream at Ragged Point or grab a bite/drink at Schooners	Wild Coast, Sea Chest, Schooners, or Taco Temple

The southern portion of Big Sur described in this adventure is day-tripper heaven. You can drive along the gorgeous coast for a relatively easy 1.5 hours from SLO, enjoy some incredible hikes and views, watch the sun dip into the Pacific, and be home in time for dinner. On the other hand, for those who like backpacking or car camping, gear up! Once in Big Sur, you will want to stay the night. Like I've said before, prices in Big Sur can be astronomical, so consider bringing your own food/supplies, and definitely gas up before you go.

Start your day with brekkie at home or make a quick stop on Main Street in Cambria at The Spot (9am–5pm), which has fresh fruit and a delicious assortment of toasts (avocado, banana, strawberry, etc.), crepes, bagels, and yogurt parfaits.

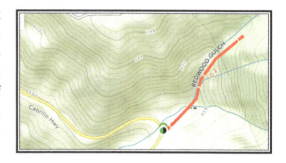

Redwood Gulch

This is a short, fun hike if you want to quickly get into the redwoods and feel like you're off the beaten path. If you search for it with Google Maps, you will be sent the wrong way; instead, search for "Nathaniel Owens Memorial Redwood Grove." You'll park on a sharp bend in the road and walk away from the water into the canyon.

There's not much to this trail as it's a simple out-and-back, but there's decent elevation gain of 374 feet over its 0.6-mile path to a peaceful little flat. This is a good spot to sit and contemplate, meditate, practice some yoga poses, or pull out a book

and read. Sometimes people camp here, but it takes away from everyone else who comes to enjoy this spot, so don't be those people. (Camper shaming is real.)

Climb up and around the redwoods to your heart's content, perhaps wander up the creek for a bit (watch out for poison oak), and when you're ready or when the path is blocked by a giant boulder and you can go no farther, head back down and on to the next stop.

Cruickshank Trail to Upper Cruickshank Camp
If you want a strong workout to begin your day, head to Cruickshank Trail and hike to Upper Cruickshank Camp. This one will get your heart pumping. It starts out very steep, gaining almost a thousand feet in the first 0.8 miles, then becomes more gradual after that. The beginning is exposed, but the views are spectacular. You'll eventually get into tree canopy. About two miles into the hike, there's a small creek where you can get water (assuming you've brought a filter). At Upper Cruickshank Camp there is one table and firepit. This is a good spot for a picnic lunch or a snack. Keep an eye out for condors riding the morning thermals upward. (I have yet to see them, but others have said this is the case.) Spend a few minutes simply listening and breathing in and out. When you feel all warm and fuzzy, you are ready to head back down to your car and on to the next stop on our adventure.

Distance:	Elevation Gain:	Difficulty:
5.2 miles	1,368 feet	Moderate

Sand Dollar Beach
Ironically, Sand Dollar Beach is almost completely devoid of sand dollars. If you go there for them, you will be disappointed. More importantly, if you want to enjoy

the beach, you should not go at high tide. Check the tides here and plan your morning accordingly: https://www.swellinfo.com/surf-forecast/tidechart/loc/enp_us_ca_big_sur. Park on Highway 1 if you want to avoid the $10 parking fee. (Guilt trip alert: the fees help support our parks.) While some reviews are mixed about this spot — mainly because the person went during high tide or expected sand dollars — at LOW tide, this is one of the biggest, best, and most accessible beaches in Big Sur. I find this approximately one-mile-long stretch of beach gorgeous and perfect for kids, beach running, exploring, and getting your feet wet. If you want a nice big beach in Big Sur, it doesn't get any better than this. Surfers, head here early in the morning before the wind picks up. If the weather is good, don't forget a frisbee. Of course, everything I just mentioned changes during high tide. At high tide, there is no beach. You can still walk along the base of the cliffs through the rock mounds, which is cool in its own way, but changes the entire experience.

As you're heading from your car to the beach, there is a great view and selfie spot at the top of the steps on the right prior to going down to the beach. Both the north and south parts of the beach are worth exploring. To the north is a cave, and the southern end has some really cool rock formations and serpentine rocks. Known as California's state rock, serpentine is greenish, brownish, and spotted. These decorative stones are a source of magnesium and asbestos. Please don't take any rocks home with you, so others can enjoy them.

Surf's up at Sand Dollar Beach

Big Sur South

You can make a loop of your beach walk by taking the trail up from the northern side of the beach rather than walking back to the steps.

Sand Dollar Beach is near the campgrounds of Plaskett Creek and Kirk Creek, both of which have some remarkable camp sites (almost always full on weekends, so make your reservations online well in advance at https://www.recreation.gov/). Many campers head to the beach during the day, but, even so, this beach is never crowded.

Sand Dollar Beach-less at high tide

Jade Cove

Next on your adventure is Jade Cove, which is very easy to miss but adds a fun thirty minutes to your day. If you're strapped for time, or traveling with younger kids, skip this one. When you see the sign for Plaskett Creek campground, you'll want to park on the ocean side of Highway 1.

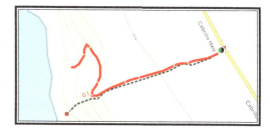

You'll need to wear proper shoes, as sandals don't work well on the rocks. Take the wooden stairs that go over the fence to the short but increasingly steep five-minute hike down to the water. You can look for jade in the rocks (sometimes between waves, so beware). You'll want to make sure the tide is somewhat out, and even so, the rocks can and probably will be slippery. Relax to the sound of the crashing waves. Leave any jade behind so that the next adventurer will have something to discover.

As you continue on your way south, there are multiple hikes along the way. Pick the one that speaks to you.

Willow Creek Picnic Area and Beach

While traveling south on Highway 1, shortly before the turnoff for Treebones Resort, you'll see a parking area on the right for a vista point. There's plenty of parking up top. To the right of the parking area there is a small, unmarked paved road down to the beach. Depending on the time of day, this is a good spot to get to sea-level quickly and watch the sun set.

Driving down the little road takes you to Willow Creek Picnic Area and Beach, which has parking for about ten cars and a tight turnaround area. This is a lovely spot where people surf, kayak, fish, or have an **EPIC** chillax sesh. There is a nice rocky beach and stream. If you have your water shoes, you can walk up the creek a bit. This is a good location for a picnic or watching the sunset.

EPIC option: I went to this spot five times before I learned that if you cross over the stream (to the right as you're facing the ocean), you'll find a "hidden" long sandy beach which you'll likely have all to yourself.

Treebones Resort

Treebones is a very cool spot where you can camp in a tent, rent a yurt, or channel your inner child and stay in a treehouse. You'll want to plan ahead, because this place fills up far in advance. Note that kids under 6 are not allowed and there are only two "family" yurts, which allow up to six people each. Everything else is two people max. They have yoga most days of the week. The store inside the main building offers lots of picnic items. There is a heated pool and small hot tub with *killer views* overlooking the ocean. There is also a restaurant with the same *killer views*. Can you think of any better way to end your day in Big Sur? In the event you booked a spot here for the night, you lucky dog, you'll probably be ready for a soak. If not, hopefully you booked a spot at the restaurant, which is easily one of the best along the Big Sur coast. If you didn't do that either, I suggest you at least walk into the main building and take a quick look around. No doubt you'll want to come back.

The pool at Treebones with Pacific views

Redwood Gulch
If you haven't done Redwood Gulch on the way up (see description earlier in the chapter), now's your chance. Otherwise, continue on to…

Salmon Creek Trail and Salmon Creek Falls
This trail is similar to Cruickshank in a lot of ways: distance, elevation gain, payoff. What differentiates this one is you can do the short hike to Salmon Creek Falls and/or opt to do the longer hike up to Spruce and Estrella Camps.

To get to the falls, you only need to walk about five to ten minutes. Stay to the left at the fork. Perhaps check out the cave under the boulder in the middle of the waterfall if you're not afraid of getting a little wet. Rumor has it that back in the late 60s/early 70s, this area housed a number of hippies and deserters from the armed forces. If you can manage to get to the boulder in the middle of the waterfall without hurting yourself, the view is great.

Big Sur South

If you want more, head back to the main trail and begin doing the switchbacks where you'll gain more than 800 feet in elevation passing through lovely scenery the entire way. After that, the trail becomes much more gradual. For a while, you will walk parallel to the creek and enjoy its soothing sounds. Near the Spruce Trail camp there is a fork — go left to stay on Salmon Creek Trail. At Estrella Camp, take a rest, then begin your journey down, which, on a clear day, rewards you with beautiful ocean views. Timing your descent with the sunset is especially gorgeous.

At this point, I'm assuming you're done for the day, but if you happen to have a little left in the tank (or you have a lot left because you've already done the other hikes on a previous trip), here is how you can also explore the southernmost area of Big Sur, starting from Ragged Point.

Ragged Point
Ragged Point is a family-run business that used to be part of Hearst Ranch. Back in the 1950s, Wiley and Milfred Ramey purchased the property and built it

Big Sur coastal view north from Ragged Point

up over the decades from a tiny snack shack with some rusted gas pumps to the sprawling 39-room hotel, restaurant, gift shop, and snack bar with locally made ice cream that it has become. The Ramey children, grandchildren, and great-grandchildren still run the property today.

At a minimum, stop at Ragged Point to use the bathroom, get ice cream, and walk around back of the property for stunning cliff views while enjoying said ice cream. The spot in the very back corner with a view up and down the coast is particularly special.

There are two hikes worth doing in Ragged Point: a short one down to the beach (during low tide only) and a longer one with *killer views*.

Ragged Point Trail to the Beach
To get to the starting point for the beach, walk past the ice cream and bathrooms to the cliffs. You will see great spots for sitting along the ledge and the steep trail that leads down to the beach. Going down is easy, but it's a steep hike back up, so you'll want to wear something better than flip-flops. Go during low to mid-tide or while the tide is going out and you'll likely have the beach to yourself. If you go at high tide, the beach will be under water and you'll almost definitely have that to yourself.

Once you ascend the trail, reward yourself with some of that ice cream if you haven't already, and grab a seat to take in the views.

Ragged Point Fire Road Trail

Like many of the other trails up from Highway 1 in Big Sur, this one is a leg-burner. You can leave your car by the restaurant, or there is public parking at the southern end of the Ragged Point property. Cross over the highway and you'll ascend for a few miles. There is no forest, so your views are spectacular the entire way. Once you get to the T-intersection, many people stop to take in the views, then head back down. Don't make that mistake! If you go just a little farther, you'll be rewarded. Go right at the intersection for about 200 yards, then follow the faint path into the fields to the right. Look for a dead tree at the top of the hill and head to that spot. The views are spectacular! On a clear day, you can see all the way to the lighthouse. Travel back down the way you came and enjoy sensational views the entire way.

Congratulations — you just had an amazing day in Big Sur! Check the previous adventures for eating recommendations from here as you head south. You're probably hungry verging on hangry, so consider stopping in Cambria, Cayucos, or Morro Bay (Taco Temple) for dinner.

San Simeon Day Trip

Top Tourist Attraction on the Central Coast ... For Good Reason!

What to Bring: hat, sunscreen, water, picnic
When to Go: Anytime
Duration/Distance: A minimum of 4 hours

Directions to Start: Take Highway 1 from SLO — it goes directly to San Simeon

Adventure Agenda	Option 1	Option 2
Breakfast	The Spot in Cambria	Eat at home
Morning Adventure	Hearst Castle	Piedras Blancas Light Station
Lunch/Afternoon	Hearst Ranch Winery or picnic Hearst Beach and/or San Simeon Bay Trail	Elephant Seal Rookery Hearst Ranch Winery or picnic at beach
Late Afternoon	Elephant Seal Rookery	Hearst Castle
Sunset	Moonstone Beach (Cambria)	Moonstone Beach (Cambria)
Dinner	Sea Chest Restaurant and Oyster Bar	Linn's

Start your day by eating a quick bite at home or having a healthy brekkie in Cambria. If you have reservations at Piedras Blancas Light Station, follow most of option 2 above. If not, follow option 1 above. San Simeon and Hearst Castle are practically synonymous. If you've never been to Hearst Castle, you are guaranteed to be impressed. This is a can't-miss destination!

Hearst Castle

The Central Coast has been changed forever because of one man — William Randolph Hearst. The bajillionaire in *Citizen Kane* is based after Hearst, the bajillionaire who made San Simeon his own private playground. At one point he had the largest private zoo in the world, and on a lucky day, you can still see zebras roaming the plains — not something you're likely to see anywhere else unless you happen to be in Africa. Hearst Castle was such a huge construction endeavor that a whole town (Cambria) grew up to support the effort. Today, Hearst Castle, designed by architect Julia Morgan, pulls in more tourists than any other attraction on the Central Coast. It's a good example of what someone would do if they had all the money in the world. Amazing? Yes, but, you know, "Rosebud."

San Simeon Day Trip

Have you ever seen a more inviting pool?

If you're planning to go to the castle, especially during the summer or on a weekend, you have to book ahead (http://hearstcastle.org/). The recommended tour for first-timers is the Grand Rooms tour. If you've done that one, I'd recommend any tour that puts you up at the castle during sunset — the view over the open land and Pacific is nothing short of spectacular. Time permitting, it's a good idea to watch the movie in the Visitor Center prior to your tour so you get some context on what you're about to see. The day tours include full access to roam the grounds. I could sit near that pool all day long, but don't even think about dipping your toes! I know you want to, you little devil, but don't — or you'll get a hefty ticket (as they will be quick to tell you). Between the tour, the bus rides up and down the hill, and walking the grounds, you should plan to spend at least a minimum of two hours at the castle, but it's more likely you'll spend three. As such, I like to book my trips first thing in the morning so I can be back in time for lunch. No food is available once you get on the bus up to the castle and they don't allow you to bring food with you. You can bring your own (reusable) bottle of water.

Piedras Blancas Light Station

If you happen to be a fan of lighthouses, you would probably enjoy a tour of the Piedras Blancas Light Station. You'll need to look online and book ahead since tours only happen a few times a week. At this writing, tour times are 9:45 a.m. ONLY on Tuesdays, Thursdays, and Saturdays. Tours are approximately two hours long. If you wanted to do this on the same day as Hearst Castle, see option 2 at the beginning of the chapter. You'll want to rearrange things so that you start all the way north and go in this order: Lighthouse, Elephant Seal Rookery, Hearst Ranch Winery for lunch, Hearst Castle tour, San Simeon Bay Trail, dinner in Cambria.

Lunch

For lunch, you have a few options, or should I say *few* options? You can either eat at the Hearst Castle Visitor Center, which is your typical overpriced and underwhelming tourist fare, OR, if that doesn't sound thrilling, go across the street to the Hearst Ranch Winery which is an absolute gem overlooking the San Simeon State Beach. Bonus, the food is delicious and reasonably priced. The beef is free-range and comes from one of the two largest suppliers on the Central Coast. Make sure you make a reservation (11am – 4pm) online, especially on the weekends or you'll have no chance to get one of the coveted tables. If the food and the view aren't enough for you, the wines are good too and I like knowing they're bottled right there in San Simeon. **SLOcals Only Pro Tip:** If you don't get a reservation, they will usually allow you to order food to go which along with a bottle of wine or some of the cheese and meats they sell make for an absolutely perfect picnic down on the beach.

Time to work off some of that beef? Drive a few minutes south from Sebastian's to what was Hearst's pier and beach.

Hearst Castle State Beach

This lovely stretch of sand used to be where treasures from all over the world made their way up to Hearst Castle. Nowadays, it's a wonderful place to take a walk on the beach or out on the pier. On the beach is Kayak Outfitters, a kayak tour company, that offers delightful tours out to sea. If you don't want to kayak, enjoy this superb stretch of beach or explore the great trail just north of the beach.

San Simeon Day Trip

View of San Simeon State Beach from beginning of San Simeon Bay Trail

San Simeon Bay Trail

The San Simeon Bay Trail is a gorgeous, family-friendly trail. Bring a layer as it can get windy. This 4.3-mile out and back follows the cliffs and has a few areas where you can drop down to the water (mainly during low tide, check the tide tables).

You will need to walk about a quarter mile along the beach north of the San Simeon Pier until you see a wide trail cutting up the hill on the right. This is the main trail.

Like most Central Coast hikes, note there can be poison oak and ticks. The views are great and so is the cypress grove you'll walk through. The trail is wide, and therefore solid for trail running and easy for kids. But don't make the mistake of thinking it's completely safe for kids — the hike goes along the cliffs, so if your kids are overly clumsy or daredevils, it might have you on edge. (See what I did there?) There are multiple hidden beaches you can have to yourself. The long stretch of beach at the end is especially fantastic. If you're extra lucky, you may see elephant seals here. This area also doubles as the turnaround point.

Elephant Seal Rookery

Did someone say "blubber time"? Yes, I did. Grab your camera and head a few minutes north to the Elephant Seal Rookery by Piedras Blancas and turn off on the ocean side of Highway 1 for the viewing areas for elephant seals. From about December through June, you can witness the spectacle of hundreds of sea lions along the beach wallowing around over one another, molting, bellowing, fighting, and generally carrying on like our politicians in Washington! Did I mention they stink, too? Not the sea lions, the politicians! ***SLOcals* Only Pro Tip**: As you're heading back south of the viewing area with the vista point sign, look on the right for a small shoulder area that has a

trail leading down to the ocean. At times you may get your own private elephant seal viewing area. Stay back though — those beasts can crush you in the blink of an eye!

Dinner

Hangry? Get on the 1 and start going south toward civilization. If you want great seafood, head for the pricey-yet-delish Sea Chest Restaurant and Oyster Bar. They have the best waiting area in the region, but know that a line forms at 5 p.m. for their 5:30 p.m. open time and they only take cash and check. You are almost guaranteed a wait, so if you want to feel really smart, you'll get there an hour before you want to eat to enjoy a bottle of wine with an ocean view while you wait for your table. You can thank me later.

Before heading home, you might want a sweet little souvenir. If so, head over to Linn's Easy As Pie and grab one of the best pies in the region. Many go for the Olallieberry. Personally, I'm fond of the pecan. Can you think of a sweeter way to end an **EPIC** day? Me neither!

San Simeon sunset

Cambria and Harmony

Relaxation, Simplicity, Beauty, and Taking It Slow

What to Bring: hat, sunscreen, water, picnic, your favorite book
When to Go: Anytime
Duration/Distance: A few hours or all day

Directions to Start: Drive north from SLO about 34 miles on Highway 1

Adventure Agenda	Option 1	Option 2
Breakfast	Eat at home	The Spot in Cambria
Morning Adventure	Harmony Headlands Trail and town of Harmony	Fiscalini Ranch Preserve
Brunch	Gourmet: Sow's Ear Cafe, Linn's Restaurant, Robin's Restaurant Walk around town	Greasy Spoon: Redwood Café or the Creekside Garden Walk around town
Afternoon	Stepladder Creamery Moonstone Beach	Nitt Witt Ridge
Sunset	Fiscalini Ranch Preserve	Moonstone Beach
Dinner	Linn's, Robin's, Madeline's	Sea Chest Oyster Bar and Seafood Restaurant

I always thought of Cambria as a pleasant, sleepy, artsy, and romantic little retirement town nestled in Monterey pine trees, and, for the most part, that's pretty accurate. This adventure does not have challenges that will make you question your sanity, but if you want a quaint town that is perfect for brunch, arguably the best beach along the entire Central Coast and multiple ways to stretch your legs, with a *killer view* to boot, you will enjoy this day. Even adventure hounds need an easy day every once in a while, right?

Cambria is somewhat split into two parts. The village of Cambria is very walkable, slightly inland from the ocean and east of Highway 1. The coastal part of Cambria is west of Highway 1 and is mainly houses interrupted by the Fiscalini Ranch Preserve, with one commercial area along Moonstone Beach. If the weather is cold near the water, go inland to the village where it will likely be warmer.

Cambria is a great place to visit at different times of year, as the feel of this area changes with the seasons. For instance, in spring, the hills are green, the wildflowers are blooming, and you will feel like you've dropped into a Dutch village. Early summer and fall bring almost perfect weather. Fall is also a great time to do an evening tour at nearby Hearst Castle or check out the Scarecrow Festival in October. In winter, there's the Art & Wine Festival and what will likely be your favorite — the Cambria Christmas Market light show, which runs from Thanksgiving to Christmas and requires tickets, which typically sell out. To find out what is happening during your visit, check the Cambria events calendar at: https://visitcambriaca.com/events.

Heading north from SLO on the 1, your first option for the day will be about five miles past Cayucos: The Headlands Trail in Harmony Headlands State Park.

Harmony Headlands Trail

I'm going to be honest: This isn't one of my favorite trails, as it's basically a long dirt road to the ocean. But this 4.3-mile out-and-back is easy, kid-friendly, and flat enough to bring a stroller. Many people really like this walk for the solitude and beauty. So, I leave the choice up to you. Personally, I'd skip it unless you've never done it before or you're yearning for a long walk to the ocean for viewpoints similar to what you'll see later in Cambria.

A row of pelicans fly along Harmony Headlands Trail

Parking is on the west side of Highway 101; while heading north, the best mile marker is the billboard on the right advertising Linn's Easy As Pie Cafe. Immediately after, turn off on the left into the parking lot.

The best time to do this trail is in the spring during the wildflower bloom. If you do it first thing in the morning, you'll likely have it all to yourself.

Harmony

Next, you will come to the cozy little town of Harmony. Population: 18. And that might be stretching it. Blink and you'll miss it, as the town is only comprised of a few buildings that are partially obscured by foliage. Harmony is a fun stop, partially because it has the most pleasant

name of just about anywhere, and also because there are some enjoyable shops, including one where you can see glassblowers at work. There's also Harmony Cellars, a nice place to grab a glass of wine.

Cambria

Continuing on to Cambria, take the first entrance to town on the right from Highway 1 on Main Street. Cambria has an east side and a west side. The east side is the downtown area and the west side is more like traveling through an old European village. First go to the east side. I usually park in the center, right around Main Street and Bridge Street. Of all the places on the Central Coast, this might be *the* town for breakfast and brunch. If you want gourmet food, have brunch at the Sow's Ear Cafe, Linn's Restaurant, or my favorite, Robin's Restaurant. For more of a greasy spoon, head slightly west to the Redwood Café or the Creekside Garden, both of which will deliver a solid traditional breakfast. Head slightly farther west for good coffee at Lily's Coffee House or the lovely Seed & Sow, which also has several nice outside areas for taking your morning easy.

Take a walking tour of the downtown area, which includes antique stores, art galleries, restaurants, clothing, and sweets shops. The heart of the East Village is near the French Corner Bakery near the corner of Main Street and Burton Drive. Park just about anywhere nearby. Make sure you stop in at Phil Hauser

Art & Design on 2068 Main Street, where you can watch artists at work and purchase local art. If you are putting together a picnic for later, Soto's True Earth Market next to the bakery is where you want to go.

If you'd like a mid-morning tour, you have two fun and completely different options. Do you like cheese or do you like crazy? Each will require a short drive.

Stepladder Creamery
For the cheese fans, about two miles out of town you'll find Stepladder Creamery, a small goat farm and creamery that offers one-hour tours of the grounds, complete with tastings of about a dozen delectably fresh goat's and cow's milk cheeses. The creamery is open to the public, but by appointment only (the gates are locked so don't try to drop by). Call ahead at 858-336-2479.

Nitt Witt Ridge
Did you choose crazy over cheese? If so, keep track of your time, because every hour on the hour from 10 a.m. to 5 p.m., there is a strange, not-to-be-missed tour of one of the weirdest houses you'll ever see located in the West Village. And the name is … Nitt Witt Ridge.

Cambria and Harmony

Nitt Witt Ridge at 881 Hillcrest Dr, Cambria, CA, is a crazy journey into the mind of Arthur Harold Beal (aka Captain Nitt Witt), a garbage collector who took the idea that "one man's trash is another man's treasure" quite literally. He spent fifty years building his "castle on the hill" using his neighbors' discarded toilet seats, bathtubs, abalone shells, tire rims, and beer cans (after being consumed, of course). There are about six roadside parking spots just outside the house. To tour, show up and wait.

Picnic Fixins

If you toured Nitt Witt Ridge, you may need to walk off some of that crazy. Which is good, because it's time for a walk. But you can't go without rations, right? Let's put together a killer picnic.

If you like a drink with lunch, head to 927 Beer, Cambria's only brewery, and get a few 22s or a bottle of wine across the street (screw-off cap and don't forget the cups) at Moonstone Cellars. You should probably grab one extra for later tonight. Next, get a delectable treat at the hard-to-find Red Moose Cookie Company. All of their cookies are fantastic, so you really can't go wrong. **Slocals Only Pro-Tip**: Ask if they have any Naughty Rods. This secret item sells out so quick, they don't display it. But rest assured, it is one of the greatest desert inventions of our time — but only if you like pretzels, caramel, dark chocolate, nuts, and love. You probably already went to Soto's True Earth Market in the East Village, which has great picnic fixins; if not, you can head there now. Or, if you want a prepared lunch, head to Sandy's Deli and Bakery in the West Village.

Treat from Red Moose

Now that you have some grub, let's head to the beach!

Moonstone Beach
Moonstone Beach is the best spot for walking in Cambria and is sure to please even the most grumpy or lazy in your group. It is an easy 2.8-mile round-trip walk along the coast that is family-, dog- (on leash), and age-friendly. Talk about friendly! There is a boardwalk you can use the entire time, which is great if you want to run or if you have a stroller. Bikes, however, are not permitted. There is free parking on the north and south sides, and you can start from anywhere. I prefer to start from the south. From Highway 1, go west at Windsor Boulevard and take the immediate right onto Moonstone Beach Drive. There is plenty of parking on your left just past the El Colibri Hotel & Spa. The trail begins on the left. There are plenty of spots to sit on a bench and enjoy the view, watch the surf, and the surfers. I like to drop down to the beach at the first stair entrance and after getting into the sand, turn right. The beach goes for a bit and comes to a point, which is about the halfway point. From here, you round the bend for an equally long stretch of beach. Make a structure with driftwood, search for moonstones, and have a picnic. If you want to do the entire walk, eventually make your way back up to the boardwalk and follow it as it takes you past the bridge and up onto a bluff. In the event you want to stay overnight, there are a number of hotels just inland that offer great access to this trail.

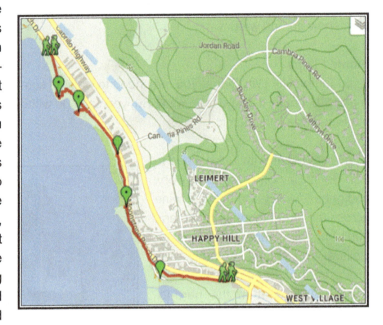

Find rocks every color of the rainbow on Moonstone Beach

Most people will tell you that a trip to Cambria isn't complete without going north to check out Hearst Castle. If you only have one day to check out the area, I agree, that has to be on your itinerary. Even the most well-traveled European will find something awe-inspiring there. In this book, I give San Simeon and Hearst Castle their own adventure (#12), so check that out if you want to head up north. For now, let's go see another jewel of Cambria.

Fiscalini Ranch Preserve
If you liked the Moonstone Beach walk, chances are good you are going to enjoy the Bluff Trail in the Fiscalini Ranch Preserve. This space was preserved through one family's desire to avoid taxes and the city's foresight to restrict development. Now you get to enjoy the fruit of their labor.

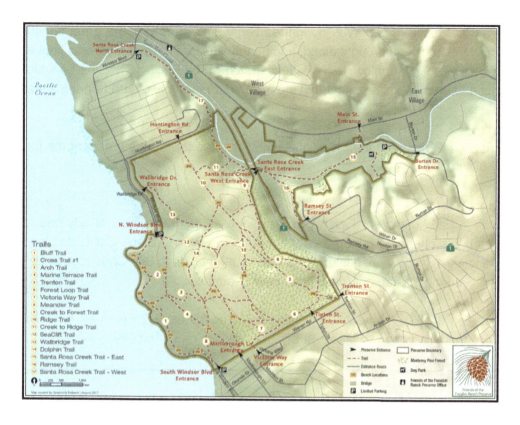

To get to the Fiscalini Ranch Preserve, drive southwest on Windsor Boulevard from Highway 1. The road wraps south past Shamel Park (kid- and dog-friendly park where you can unwind, go to the beach, play horseshoes, or have a picnic) then continues along the water to a parking area at Abalone Cove. There are numerous trails in all directions. The trail outlined here is approximately 2.4 miles and is a nice option. So,

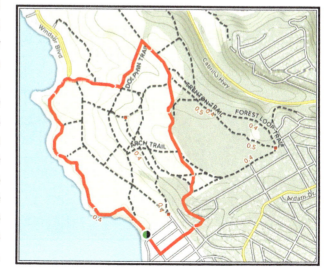

Cambria and Harmony

grab that bottle of wine you bought earlier, wander freely, find a great bench, enjoy the book you brought along, and be thankful that development was kept at bay so we can all enjoy such a lovely stretch of the Pacific. This is a beautiful place to enjoy a sunset, so if that's part of your plan, make sure to bring some layers.

Thanks to Friends of the Fiscalini Ranch Preserve for the great map at the top of this section.

Dinner
Starving? I thought so. Finish your day with a memorable meal at any one of Cambria's charming restaurants. I'm partial to Robin's, Black Cat Bistro, and Madeline's. If you want ocean views with your meal, go to Sea Chest Oyster Bar and Seafood Restaurant (cash only) prior to sunset.

Can you think of a time when walking 5+ miles felt easier? Fresh air, serenity, good food, and ocean walks … that's the makings of a great day.

The northern tip of Moonstone Beach

14
Cayucos and Estero Bluffs
Best Beach Town in California (Yup, I said it.)

What to Bring: hat, sunscreen, water, snacks, lightweight beach blanket, swimsuit, sunglasses, warm layer, water shoes
When to Go: Anytime, low tide for the bluffs
Duration/Distance: 20–30 minutes driving each way, all day to play

Directions to Start: From SLO, head north on Highway 1. Get off at Cayucos Drive and drive through town. Park near Ocean & Cayucos Drive.

If you're from out of town, your favorite Central Coast beach town is likely Pismo Beach or maybe lesser-known northwestern neighbor Avila Beach. Somehow, Cayucos has stayed under the radar. For locals, Cayucos reigns supreme. Named one of the "coolest small towns" in the U.S. by Frommer's Budget Travel Magazine, this place isn't trying to be a tourist destination — it's a town first, and that means livability is more important than drawing in ever more tourists. There is not as much to do as the other beach towns in the area, but that's the point. This is a beach town reminiscent of what California once was: a bunch of disparate small towns with their own hearts and souls. It feels a bit like going to the Old West, but by the beach. Not many towns like this exist in California anymore, so consider yourself lucky and enjoy this one while you can.

To get you in the mood, listen to a California band from Santa Monica who named themselves Cayucas after the town. Look up "Cayucos" by Cayucas, which captures the vibe of the town perfectly. The song also has a great music video, which was mainly filmed in SoCal. But can you spot the scenes from the real town?

If you plan to do the Estero Bluffs today, google "Cayucos tides" before leaving for your adventure to find when low tide occurs so you can to head to the trail one to two hours before that time.

Morning in Cayucos

Start your day with a quick bite and coffee from either Top Dog Coffee or Luna Coffee Bar. In the back of Luna is Lunada Garden Bistro, which has a really pleasant patio/garden area — a lovely setting for any meal. They have a delicious Sunday brunch beginning at 9 a.m. If you really want to feel like you're on vacation, do as we did: get some breakfast and start with dessert. How many times have you done that in your life? Not many, I'm guessing. The Waffles A La Mode is everything your parents didn't want you to eat in the morning: waffles that are basically like fried doughnuts, topped with berries, whipped cream, and two scoops of ice cream. It's enough sugar to kill a man, so make sure you bring a friend. The Mexican Cappuccino or latte is also great. **SLOcals Only Pro Tip**: Call ahead to get reservations, and if you're extra lucky, you'll be able to reserve the hidden garden table for four.

The perfect spot for brunch: Lunada's back patio

Now that you're sufficiently hopped up on caffeine and sugar, call your parents or someone else's parents and tell them they were right about that whole starting the day with sugar thing ... then walk your way through your sugar crash as you see the town. Ocean Boulevard is the main drag, so you'll want to stroll up and down both sides of the street. I like to combine the downtown walk with the murals spread around town.

Waffles A La Mode

Murals? Yes, thanks to The Cayucos Mural Society, founded in 1992, there are nine high-quality murals around town. The murals are based on Cayucos history and are scattered both inside and outside the buildings.

Cayucos and Estero Bluffs

Here's a trusty, interactive map of the murals, courtesy of The Cayucos Mural Society: http://www.cayucos.org/muralsociety/virtualtour.html

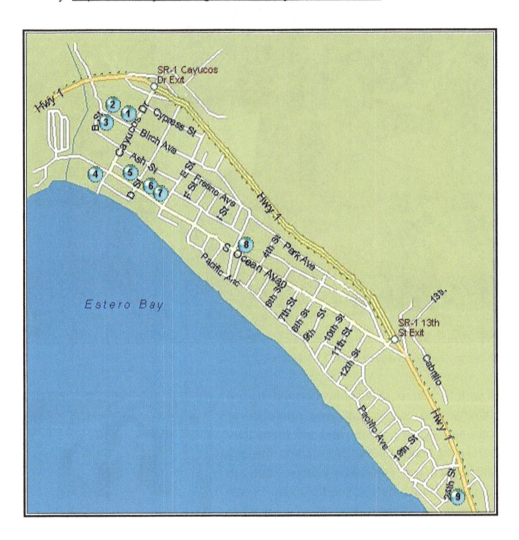

Since you're currently in the thick of it, start in the middle of the tour at mural #4, located on the northwest corner of Cayucos Drive and Ocean Avenue, which also happens to be conveniently near the public bathrooms. Head out on the pier and get *killer views* in all directions. Back from the pier, head to Ocean and hang a right. You will quickly pass Schooners — one of the best seafood spots and bars — then Café Della Via, which has solid Italian fare.

There are lots of cool shops to check out, including Cayucos Collective, a great shirt and hat shop that can create custom attire for you in five minutes. Continuing on, you'll pass Paul's Liquor, which has a terrific assortment of beer. File that one for later. Toward the ocean from Paul's is Ruddell's Smokehouse, which, if you like smoked fish tacos, will be your new happy place. Any picnic is kicked up several notches with fish tacos. Continue walking on the side of the street toward the ocean, and once you reach E Street, you can cross over to the side of the street with Top Dog Coffee.

Mural #7 is supposedly on the south side of the antique store Remember When Too. I can't find the mural to save my life, but the shop is worth checking out.

Continuing back toward the center of town, just past the windmill, you will see Mural #6, which depicts a horse-drawn delivery of goods.

Assuming you have already enjoyed Lunada Garden Bistro, you absolutely have to stop at Brown Butter Cookie Company. It's a Cayucos staple and has now expanded into Paso and SLO, but this is the original. Those tiny morsels of buttery love are too delicious to pass up and they are highly unique. If you want to be popular anywhere you go, bring a bag of these along as a gift, then bask in the glow of your smiling new best friends. Grab one or two or a dozen cookies for your afternoon hike.

Mural spotting in Cayucos

You next will pass the Old Cayucos Tavern, which, pavement aside, looks like it should have horses tied up out front and some villainous outlaw flying through the front window. Inside, you will find Mural #5.

Cayucos and Estero Bluffs

A few doors down is another worthwhile antique shop, the original Remember When. "Shirley" a treasure awaits inside. If your name is not Shirley, I make no guarantees.

At the gas station, look toward the back — this is where you can find a hidden Mexican food joint that, as the long lines suggest, is worth a stop. Score extra cheap tacos on Taco Tuesday.

Cross over to Cass House, the home of the original founder of Cayucos. There's been several additions over the years, including a bakery, a bar, and a spacious outdoor area where large groups can enjoy their food and drinks. Some of the best food in town can be found within the house. This also makes for a pleasant lunch spot.

If you want to see more murals, you can walk to 1, 2, and 3, but for 8 and 9, you'll probably want to bike or drive. A brief description of where to find each: From Cayucos Drive and Ocean Avenue, head toward Highway 1 (away from the ocean). Mural #1 is located at Cayucos Elementary School within the school grounds. Be sure to check in at the office if school is in session. Make a right turn at the school onto Birch and proceed down the hill. On your right will be Mural #2.

Turn left on B Street and on the left is Mural #3, the mosaic sculpture. Mural #8 is off of Ocean Avenue, located at the corner of 3rd Street on the parking lot side of the Cayucos Super Market, about five blocks farther south than Top Dog Coffee. Continue south on Ocean Avenue to 13th Street and turn right. Go two blocks to Pacific Avenue and turn left. Pacific will dead-end at 24th Street. Turn left and Mural #9 will be the second house on your right. This is a private residence.

For me, no trip to Cayucos is complete without grabbing some cookies from Brown Butter Cookie Company, some fish tacos from Ruddell's, and a tasty beverage or two from Paul's Liquors, and taking my whole bounty down to the ocean to grub. You can choose to hit the beach in town or grab a picnic and do the walk along the Estero Bluffs. For those who like their food served on a table, it's tough to beat the view from Schooners Wharf. If you happen to go to the upstairs bar, the views might just keep you there all afternoon. Don't say I didn't warn you.

If the water is calling to you, head over to Good Clean Fun to rent a surfboard, boogie board, or kayak. If you're not a surfer, now's your chance — they also offer surf lessons, and Cayucos is a great place to learn.

If you're a fan of long walks on the beach, you could walk/run the whole way to Morro Rock. Otherwise, consider doing a little more of a hike just north of town at the Estero Bluffs.

Estero Bluffs

Now that you're sufficiently fed and feeling good, and probably loving Cayucos, it's time to venture out, because the area around Cayucos is fantastic, too! A killer coastline awaits just north of town at Estero Bluffs State Park. The 353-acre park hugs the shoreline and is filled with easy walking trails, tide pools, completely empty beaches, lots of sea life, great rockhounding, and even a sunken ship! This walk

Ruddell's Smokehouse, a must do

The shipwreck at Estero Bluffs

is most fun during low tide. That way you'll have a lesser chance of getting soaked if you go down to the tide pools. Always keep a lookout for rogue waves, though.

The simplest trailhead is accessed by driving north (the ocean is on your left) on Ocean Avenue out of town and pulling into the dirt parking lot just before you get to Highway 1. There aren't any facilities in the park, so make sure you have what you might need for several hours, including snacks, sunscreen, layers (it can be really windy), and water. Some people like to use a walking stick. Stay on the trails, as many people report ticks in the field. I'm not sure if this is a scare tactic, but I'd err on the side of no ticks.

This 4.2-mile hike is absolutely stunning. There are countless birds and you may also see sea otters, sea lions, and whales. The tide pools are teeming with zillions of hermit crabs and other forms of life. The view back toward Cayucos and Morro Bay is fantastic and fills you with energy. This is what the California coast looked like prior to all the development. Magnificent, right? Best of all, there's almost no one here. Many people like to turn around at the large beach called Estero Bay.

To make your day even more **EPIC**, watch the sun sink into the Pacific from the bluffs (near your car unless you have a flashlight) and then head back to town.

Wonderful views along the Estero Bluffs

Cayucos and Estero Bluffs

If the timing isn't quite right for the sunset, check out any of the restaurants back in the center of town. Perhaps warm up with Duckie's clam chowder or get seafood at Bill & Carol's Sea Shanty. A drink from the Schooners upstairs bar as the sun goes down is really tough to beat.

Before heading home from your amazing day in Cayucos, take one last look at the ocean and perhaps replay that Cayucas song while thinking to yourself how you might have just fallen in love.

A private beach awaits at the Estero Bluffs

Morro Bay City Tour and Urban Hike

15

The Perfect Day in Morro Bay

What to Bring: hat, sunscreen, water, picnic, binoculars
When to Go: Anytime
Duration/Distance: A few hours to all day

Directions to Start: Take Highway 1 toward Morro Rock and park along Embarcadero near the water.

With its iconic extinct volcano known as "the Rock", 3 towers and enormous bay for kayaking, boating, birding, SUPing and surfing, Morro Bay has something for everyone. As an active fishing port, there is no shortage of great spots to enjoy fresh seafood with an ocean view. If that's not enough to entice you, everyone I've ever met from Morro Bay loves it there. There is a ton to do in Morro Bay so let's get going!

Ready for a hike and/or an easily accessible view up and down the coastline as far as one can see? Perhaps grab a wrap or smoothie at Goddess Goods, grab a delicious açaí bowl at Kravabowl, or get some picnic fixins at Shine Cafe. If you favor a greasy spoon, head to Frankie & Lola's Front Street Café. Get there early or be prepared to wait. Another great option, conveniently located a few hundred yards from the trailhead, is Bayside Café. Now its time to walk off that breakfast on a terrific hike with a view.

Black Hill Trail

Head to Black Hill Trail in Morro Bay State Park. There are multiple spots where you can access the mountain. For the long hike (2.3 miles), avoid the fee and park across from the state park campground parking lot. For the short hike (0.75 miles), and/or a great viewpoint, take Park View Road through the golf course and go up the appropriately named Black Hill Road. Park at the trailhead above the golf course, which doubles as a beautiful viewpoint for those who don't have time or don't want to hike. It's also an easy way to get almost to the top in the event you're willing to hike but not too far. Black Hill is the second of the Nine Morros spanning Morro Bay to SLO. Guess which Morro is the first? Morro Rock, of course! Morro Rock is a peregrine falcon sanctuary, and you'll get thrown in jail if you try to climb it. And believe me, I know how bad you want to climb it. But Black Hill Trail is one of five Morros you *are* allowed to hike, so let's get back to that.

View of the bay from Black Hill Trail

Black Hill Trail can be too foggy, too hot, too buggy ... or it can be utterly beautiful, with outstanding 360-degree views that encompass the seven-mile stretch of

Morro Bay City Tour and Urban Hike

Sandspit Beach, Morro Bay, Morro Rock, and Cayucos on one side, and then rolling hills and gorgeous open space back toward SLO on the other. You'll only know if you go.

This relatively easy, dog-friendly hike can be done in a few hours. It takes you through Fleming's Forest, named for John Fleming, a park superintendent who planted the trees. Thank you, John! The Monterey Pine trees give way to a sweet view.

Also note that the trail is good but not well marked, so grab a map at the Morro Bay State Park ranger's station or take a picture from one of the trailheads. Also, stay away from the red and green glossy leaves all around the trail near ground level — this is poison oak and is prevalent throughout this hike.

If you did the long hike, consider taking the scenic route back by going around the mountain on your way down. For this extended option, take Powerline Trail to the Pipeline Trail to a brief stint on Exercise Trail ... then Grove Trail to Exercise Trail and back to where you started. (Just listing all the names of those trails was a hike!) Basically, stay on the east side of the trail map as much as you can. This has the extra bonus of giving you more exercise and minimizing how many people you'll see on the trail.

Morro Bay City Tour and Urban Hike

Tour of Morro Bay

I've laid out this section with the expectation that you will be walking, but know that if you do the entire walk from the state park, it'll be at least 6–7 miles. Your other option is to do some of the walk by the state park, then drive somewhere along the Embarcadero.

Full walking instructions: From the Morro Bay State Park parking lot, head south to the small but very worthwhile Museum of Natural History. Continuing north on Main Street (ocean is on your left), you will quickly walk to the Heron and Cormorant Rookery at 20 State Park Road. Time to pull out your binoculars and look to the trees next to the Inn at

Morro Bay City Tour and Urban Hike

Morro Bay. Depending on the time of year, you may see nothing, or you may see Great Blue Herons, egrets, and Double Crested Cormorants all at the same time!

Keep on walking along Main Street until you come to Olive Street, then go left toward the water for Embarcadero Street. At this corner, keeping the water on your left, walk along Embarcadero to see the main drag. Within a block you will see the Morro Bay Skateboard Museum, which is very cool if you're into that sort of thing.

For great seafood, there is no shortage of oceanside restaurants in Morro Bay. While I typically prefer my fish grilled rather than fried, it seems like every time we have folks visiting from out of town and take them for the fried seafood platter at Tognazzini's Dockside Too, that is the one restaurant they remember and want to visit again. It doesn't hurt that the place overlooks the water. And since Morro Bay (and Avila) are fishing towns, you can get fresh seafood here that was caught the same day. When I want my seafood as fresh as it gets, I head to Giovanni's Fish Market, where they also serve up food at their window. Once crab season hits (mid-November – mid-February), this is also where you can get live Dungeness crab.

Are you feeling energetic and ready to enjoy one of the top highlights in Morro Bay? If so, and if the weather is decent, you may want to kayak or stand-up paddleboard (SUP). With miles of calm waters teeming with sea life, Morro Bay is one of the best places in California to ocean kayak and explore. There are several good kayak shops along the Embarcadero (see adventure #17).

Not in the mood to kayak? When was the last time you flew a kite? With an incredibly convenient location just prior to Morro Rock, Farmer's Kites Surreys and More (1108 Front Street) has great options. From there, walk a few more minutes to Morro Rock. Continue past the Rock to fly your kite, enjoy a walk on the beach (see adventure #16), or you may be ready for a nearby hike…

Curious friends await in Morro Bay

Hike/Walk Options

If a hike is calling your name, there are three good options nearby: one really easy, one easy, and the other a bit harder. You will need to drive to get to any of the options.

Elfin Forest (Really Easy)

The really easy trail is the Elfin Forest, which is farther south on Bay Boulevard, then west (toward the ocean) on Santa Ysabel Road. You can park at the end (go north) of just about any streets from 17th down to 11th. The trail is only about a mile loop and has wonderful views of the estuary. If you want really fantastic views without having to put in much effort, this walk is for you.

Crespi Trail (Easy)

For the easy trail, use your GPS to find Crespi Trail, located off Bay Boulevard as you head south toward Los Osos. The trailhead is a small turnoff from the main road and very easy to miss. The trail is a 2.9-mile lightly used loop with cool rocks, beautiful wildflowers (especially in the spring), and nice views over Los Osos, the Sandspit, and the Bay. This is a great hike for kids, as it is varied yet mostly flat, with a few small uphill climbs. The terrain changes from meadows to forest and makes for a pleasant way to see a different side of Morro Bay.

Cerro Cabrillo (Easy/Hard)

Now for your harder hike option: Cerro Cabrillo, one of the nine Morros. I hesitate to call this hike hard because it's actually pretty easy most of the way, but then … near the end, it becomes a scramble on loose rocks to the peak. The trail is about 2.3 miles with almost 800 feet of elevation gain and features beautiful wildflowers and cool rock formations. This is also one of the best options for outdoor rock climbing in the region.

Great views from the top of Cerro Cabrillo

Dinner (And a Sunset?)
Finishing your day in Morro Bay, you will probably want to have seafood on the water if you haven't already. I already mentioned a lot of great options, but many people also like either The Galley Seafood Grill or Windows On the Water for great food and sunsets. If seafood isn't your bag, get your Mexican fix at Taco Temple, which gets my vote for the best Mexican food for 25 miles in any direction.

More Morro Bay Options
But wait, there's more! Morro Bay has so much to offer, it's impossible to do it all in one day. If you want to learn to sail, this is the place. If you want to go on a bay tour or go deep-sea fishing, you can do that. Stand-up paddle boarding, yep, got that too. Like shopping or thrift shops? Head up and down Pacific Street and Morro Bay Boulevard. Finally, make your **EPIC** day in Morro Bay even **EPIC**er by catching a band at The Siren or Stax Bar, or simply enjoy a movie at the Bay Theater.

Morro Bay City Tour and Urban Hike

Morro Rock, its even more impressive in person

Morro Rock to Cayucos (And Back) 16

Flat, Lovely 10k on Beach

What to Bring: hat, sunscreen, water, a good book, snacks
When to Go: Anytime
Duration/Distance: 6.7 miles one way with optional 6.7-mile return

Directions to Start: Drive to Morro Rock at the northern point of Embarcadero

There are not many places where you can walk almost seven miles along relatively secluded flat beach that begins and ends in lovely little towns. And there are no other places like this where you can also look over your shoulder and have Morro Rock behind you. I love this walk because it has gorgeous, unobstructed coastline coupled with the challenge of walking almost seven miles in the sand.

While doable at any time, you'll want to check the tides to avoid having to detour onto the road in Cayucos, even though doing the detour still makes for a nice outing.

This walk is family-friendly, and if you're bringing really little ones, you'll want to have a kid carrier with you since most kids lose steam after a few miles.

Morro Rock to Cayucos (And Back)

Annual Kite Festival north of Morro Rock

The directions to this hike are easy: Start at Morro Rock, walk along the beach until you reach Cayucos, and then reward yourself with a meal. The beach is flat and wide at almost all points when the tide is out. If you walk near the water, you'll be on hard-pack, which makes for much easier walking than going through the soft sand. Just a couple of other things to keep in mind: There is a middle point where you will go up over a few layers of rock and the walk turns noticeably to the right. Lastly, there is only one bathroom along the way — it is around mile five and is part of the Morro Strand State Beach Day Use Area. Look for the small square structure next to the parking lot off the beach.

Do the 10k from The Rock to Cayucos

If you get tired along the path, remember you have amazing smoked tacos waiting for you at Ruddell's Smokehouse, which has been churning out mouthwatering tacos since 1980. And no trip to Cayucos is complete without grabbing a few cookies from the Brown Butter Cookie Company. If you want a beer with a *killer view* of the ocean, go to Schooners Wharf and head to the bar upstairs. Nothing motivates activity like food!

I like to end the walk in Cayucos by heading to the bathroom at the beginning of the pier and next to the playground.

Morro Rock to Cayucos (And Back)

To get back to your car, the easiest way is to Uber. You can also catch the local bus, which runs approximately every three hours. Schedule info for the bus is here: http://www.slorta.org/schedules-fares/route-15/#south.

Ready for more?? You can make your day **EPIC** by turning around and walking back the way you came. You'll love watching Morro Rock grow as you approach, and the backdrop it adds to the beach is spectacular. Selfie time!

Never crowded, always welcoming between Morro and Cayucos

Morro Bay Water Sports and Beach Walk/Run

Kayak/SUP in Protected Bay and Take Your Pick of Private Beaches

What to Bring: hat, sunscreen, water, picnic, beach running shoes, layers
When to Go: Anytime (best when it's not too windy)
Duration/Distance: 2 hours to all-day paddling, with option for multiple miles of beach running or walking

Directions to Start: Drive and park by Back Bay Cafe in Morro Bay, drive toward Morro Rock ("the Rock") on Embarcadero, park after the last business anywhere on the left.

If you already embarked on adventures #15 and/or #16, you know Morro Bay is one of the Central Coast's great destinations. In this adventure, we are going to get out on the bay. You've got the option of countless miles of kayaking, stand-up paddle boarding (SUP), or boating, followed by a run or walk on the beach. And with Morro Bay's iconic rounded Morro Rock and three towers scraping its skyline, be careful or you may become enamored with the place.

Start by checking the tides since low-tide water levels can be only inches in many parts of the bay, which makes kayaking way less fun. Next, pick up a picnic lunch at Shine Cafe while deciding how much kayaking/SUPing you want to do. For a short kayak ride of about one-hour total, head down to the Embarcadero and park near Rock Kayak. I've had pleasant experiences renting from both Rock Kayak and Kayak Horizons. If you'd rather spend two hours on the water, park down by the Kayak Shack, which is next to the Back Bay Café. All rentals prices are nearly the same, so decide based on how long you want to paddle.

On to the adventure. Once in your "yak," you could paddle all day without seeing the entire bay. I'll assume you're starting south at the Kayak Shack. Start by making your way toward the mouth of the bay at the Rock, but head toward the side opposite the Rock.

You will likely see curious sea otters nearby and sea lions hanging out on a floating dock. Once you're near the mouth opposite the Rock, and before you go into the open ocean (which you probably don't want to do), beach your watercraft. Make sure you pull it up far enough that a higher tide will not cast it out to sea. It's a long walk around (see adventure

#19). Follow the beach toward the rocks. You will notice a skinny path that takes you toward the open ocean. You may need to climb over a few of the large boulders that help protect the bay's mouth.

Once near the ocean, look left for a beach with few people, if any. You have arrived at the end of the 7-mile sandspit, which can be accessed from Montaña de Oro or via watercraft. I have never seen more than six people on this beach, which goes on for as far as the eye can see. I've been here on days so foggy you can barely see the Rock or the three 450-foot stacks of the shuttered power plant, so be prepared for any type of weather.

Morro Bay Water Sports and Beach Walk/Run

At this point, you may want to run along the beach or just take a nice stroll. Hopefully, you brought a picnic. You can grab a spot just about anywhere except the area slightly inland that may be roped off to protect nesting birds. Settle in and imagine you are on your own island. Find some dunes to climb and slide down. Run and jump like a kid. Yell out since there is no one around to startle. This is what adventures are made of.

When you've had enough time to yourself, head back to your watercraft and either explore more of the bay (you can stop off at some of the really cool sand dune areas) or make your way back into Morro Bay. Check out adventure (#15) for suggested things to do in Morro Bay.

End your day like a pro in Morro Bay

Montaña de Oro (MDO) - The Bluff Trail

18

Soon to Be Your Favorite Walk

What to Bring: hat, sunscreen, warm jacket, headlamp, gloves, beanie
When to Go: Anytime
Duration/Distance: 2.1 miles each way with optional 16-mile adder

Directions to Start: Take Los Osos Valley Road (LOVR) from Highway 1 toward Costco and keep on going until you get near the ocean and it wraps south. Follow almost to the end and park just up the hill from Spooner's Cove.

Before you start: If you're coming in from Foothill Boulevard, drop in at Lassens (closed Sundays) to get your picnic eats. From LOVR, grab your grub at Whole Foods. Picnics are typically the way to go, and you will be winning at life if you bring a cheese plate and wine for sunset.

While Bishop Peak is the must-do hike in SLO, the Bluff Trail is the first place I tell all visitors to the SLO area they have to go if they are looking for a great walk. Its beauty cannot be understated, and the trail is easy enough for even the most out of shape (hi, Mom!). Therefore, it should be included on any SLO itinerary. We love this walk so much, we took our daughter here on a breezy and cold day when she was just nine days old. After deciding normal parents would wait until their baby was at least a solid month old, we reluctantly  returned to our car to find a warmer inland walk. What else did we learn? The weather here is very unpredictable, so be prepared for anything, and when exposed to extreme weather, nine-day-olds are total babies!

Montaña de Oro (MDO) - The Bluff Trail

This walk is a terrific example of the power of the Pacific. Just getting to this magnificent setting takes you from the rolling hills of Los Osos to a view of all of Los Osos and Morro Bay, through multiple microclimates, and finally to the awesome Pacific relentlessly crashing into the western coast of California.

Start the hike just past Spooner's Cove, which is the wide open, crescent-shaped beach with drive-up access (great spot for a beach picnic). The trailhead takes you toward the ocean. Aside from the few steps on the bridge at the very beginning, the trail is flat and off-road-stroller-friendly.

This trail takes you south along one of the most gorgeous and unique stretches of coastline you'll find in California. After walking about ten minutes, you'll come to the fingers of eroded land that reach out into the sea. Walk as far as you safely dare onto one of these fingers, especially during high tide, and listen to the waves pound into the cliff all around you. Look right (north toward the coast above Spooner's Cove) and see a series of countless fingers with water washing over them and falling back into the sea. Feel like you are in a different world? You are!

Continuing down the coastline, you have a few optional side trips. The first is down some steps to a beach and prime tide-pool area with a clearly marked sign. At low tide, it's especially fun for kids to look at the tide pools and find all types of interesting sea creatures. Farther along the trail, at the next spot where you can easily access the water, is a nice, long flat area that is just perfect for a picnic. Someone else must have thought the same thing since the table is already there waiting for you!

Montaña de Oro (MDO) - The Bluff Trail

Montaña de Oro (MDO) - The Bluff Trail

When you get to the end of the trail, you will start to curve away from the water and toward the main road. This is where most people turn around and head back. But ... if you want to upgrade this walk to an **EPIC** outing, you will make sure you do the trail between 8 a.m. to 5 p.m. Thursday through Monday from April 1 until October 31 and until 4 p.m. the rest of the year. During these times, you can follow the trail to the end, turn right at the main road, and follow the paved path toward a little wooden visitor structure down the main road. You are now on PG&E land, where the public can access 6.6 more miles of shore, but with even fewer people. This section is called Point Buchon Trail and is limited to 275 people per day. Sign in then tighten your walking or running shoes, because you have some gorgeous, relatively flat shoreline ahead of you, with nothing between you and the sea. Where else can you find this in California? That's right, nowhere! Run as far as your legs can carry you and don't give up until you see the lighthouse. If you do, well then, I guess you'll just have to come back!

Now that you know how amazing this area is, consider booking a campsite in Montaña de Oro (MDO), which is conveniently located across the street from the Bluffs trailhead. By staying in the park, you will get to linger longer and enjoy the sunset.

Montaña de Oro (MDO) - The Bluff Trail

Montaña de Oro (MDO) - The Bluff Trail

Montaña de Oro (MDO) - The Bluff Trail

Montaña de Oro (MDO) - The Bluff Trail

A Day in the Sahara: MDO Sandspit Beach

19

If the Sahara Bordered the Ocean

What to Bring: hat, sunscreen, water, picnic, layers (the weather can change quickly and get really cold)
When to Go: Anytime
Duration/Distance: 7 miles each way or 7 miles plus a few hours of kayaking

Directions to Start: From the 101, head west on Los Osos Valley Road (LOVR), which turns into Pecho Valley Road. Follow into Montaña de Oro State Park and go right for Sandspit Beach shortly after cresting a hill that provides a view back over all of Morro Bay.

If you ever wondered what it would be like to wander through the Sahara with nothing but sand for as far as the eye can see, you will love this adventure. You'll get dunes and more dunes, but you'll also get the beautiful Pacific on your left and eventually — it's no mirage — Morro Rock on the horizon.

The hike is relatively straightforward, and by that, I mean, walk straight forward,  bring plenty of water, and hike as far as you'd like. It's seven miles to the end of the sandspit. You'll have the option — and probably the calling — to head up and over the dunes to see the other side, which is Morro Bay. This little detour is farther than you think, but it's fun climbing over the dunes. Please heed any signs limiting access due to nesting birds.

A Day in the Sahara: MDO Sandspit Beach

A Day in the Sahara: MDO Sandspit Beach

The 7-mile Sandspit as seen from Black Hill in Morro Bay

A Day in the Sahara: MDO Sandspit Beach

Assuming you keep on keeping on along the sandspit and make it to the end, you will get some awesome pictures with Morro Rock as a backdrop (unless it's covered in fog). Get your selfie, then you can head back the other way. All told, you will get 14 miles of walking on the beach, and likely you will have the whole place to yourself.

To make this even more **EPIC**, find a friend (or friends) who is willing to kayak Morro Bay (see adventure #17) while you do the Sandspit, then rendezvous at the end of the Sandspit with a nice lunch together, then hand over the car keys, and switch places. The hikers now get to kayak and the kayakers now get to hike.

A good choice if you need to rent kayaks is A Kayak Shack (10 State Park Road, Morro Bay, CA 93442, open until 5 p.m.) near the Back Bay Cafe. This is pretty far south, so it means there is plenty of time for kayaking. As the kayakers hit the water and the hikers get in their cars and start off toward the trailhead, allot 2.5 hours to reunite at the tip of the Sandspit where the bay opens to the ocean.

For a little healthy competition, whoever gets back to the starting point last buys the first round of drinks at the Back Bay Café. And, if you don't know — **SLOcals Only** **Pro Tip** — the area just next to the Back Bay Café doubles as THE place to be during sunset. Now you know.

Montaña De Oro – Summit to Sea   20

Bag MDO's Highest Peak, Check Out a Beautiful Canyon, and Enjoy Spectacular Bluff Views

What to Bring: hat, sunscreen, water, picnic, layers, mountain bike, bike lock
When to Go: Anytime, but these trails are especially beautiful when the wildflowers bloom (typically February through May)
Duration/Distance: 5 hours to all day, 9.6 miles or more

Directions to Start: From the 101, head west on Los Osos Valley Road (LOVR), which turns into Pecho Valley Road, and follow into Montaña de Oro State Park.

For this adventure, you are going to tie together some of Montaña de Oro's most challenging hikes to make a 9.6-mile loop with approximately 1,800 feet of elevation gain and give yourself a bit of a "best of MDO." There are also two great variations for this day at the end of the chapter, so pick the one that calls to you.

Valencia Peak in MDO

Prior to starting your day, you may want to stop off at either Ascendo Coffee on LOVR or Celia's Garden Cafe, both conveniently located right on your way to MDO.

Montaña De Oro is one of the most gorgeous areas in SLO County and is actually one of my favorite places in California. The drive alone lets you know you're going somewhere special. As you head toward the coast, the road curves south into Montaña de Oro State Park. As you crest the first large hill, pull over for a quick minute for a *killer view* back over the sandspit reaching toward Morro Bay. Then drive through a eucalyptus grove past one of the top local surf spots.

Continuing on, you'll drive parallel to the Pacific and past the beach at Spooner's Cove. The road terminates at Bluff Trail.

View down to The Bluff Trail which hugs the coast

You'll first do the highest point in MDO — Valencia Peak — then catch Badger Trail to Rattlesnake Flats over to Coon Creek Trail, then down to the Bluff Trail to complete your loop.

Valencia Peak
The trailhead for Valencia Peak is just past Spooner's Cove and about a block past the outhouses (on the left). Park on either side of the road and take the trailhead for Valencia Peak on the left (away from the water) side of the road.

Valencia Peak is the highest peak in MDO at 1,312 feet elevation. You're starting just above sea level, so that's a pretty decent amount of elevation gain over a few miles. Weather can be tricky in MDO, and especially on this peak. On a clear day, you'll get wonderful views of Morro Bay, Cayucos, and possibly Cambria. But sometimes it's so windy, cold and foggy, you won't even see the ocean. Other times it can be brutally sunny and hot, but the views are amazing.

Start early to avoid the heat of the day, and if it's foggy, consider it part of the mystery of the place and enjoy. You'll be down by the ocean soon enough and will get your ocean views. Keep a lookout for poison oak, which is pretty common around here.

The trailhead is well marked. After about 1.5 miles, you will see Badger Trail spurs off to the south. This is the trail you'll take after doing Valencia Peak. Do the additional few miles to the top of Valencia Peak, then head back to this spot.

Badger Trail to Rattlesnake Flats to Coon Creek Trail

Badger Trail runs along the mountain at around 300–500 feet of elevation. There is a decent amount of up and down and you basically run parallel to the main road. After about 1.4 miles, you'll hit Rattlesnake Flats. If you're finished, head down to Bluff Trail and loop back. If you have more fuel in the tank, head east on Rattlesnake Flats as it winds its way back into the canyon. This stretch is lightly trafficked and deeply rewarding. Descend to Coon Creek Trail, where you have the option to extend the hike by heading as far back into the canyon as you'd like. On Coon Creek Trail, head right (west), and keep going toward the ocean. This nicely shaded and pretty path ends at the parking lot where there are bathrooms.

Rattlesnake Flats heading towards Coon Creek Trail

Bluff Trail

Now walk across the street to pick up the Bluff Trail, my #1 trail to recommend to anyone from out of town (see adventure #18). Follow Bluff Trail down to the ocean as you wander along the fingers of land stretching out into the Pacific, which are constantly pounded by waves. There are many great places to stop and snack along this stretch. I

highly recommend heading down and exploring the tide pools near the end of the hike. Continuing on, you'll come back to the main parking area where you'll find your car.

One of the many "fingers" on Bluff Trail reaching out into the Pacific

Spooner's Cove

If you're not ready to leave, drive down to Spooner's Cove and pull out your beach chairs, snacks, some of your favorite beverages, and watch the sun set into the Pacific as your magical day in MDO comes to a satisfying end.

There are two great alternatives to the Summit to Sea Loop described above. Perhaps consider one of the two options below as alternatives or add-ons for the day.

Spooner's Cove

Option 1: The EPIC Triple Bagger

The **EPIC** Triple Bagger option allows you to bag three MDO summits: Valencia Peak, Oats Peak, and Hazard Peak. It's possible to do all three peaks via foot, but you will be walking and running all day and need to be in terrific shape. Personally, I like to bike and hike. Start with the bike ride to Oats Peak and leave your bike where Oats Peak Trail meets Valencia Peak Trail so that you only need to hike the 0.5 miles to the top of Valencia Peak. Then get back on your bike and continue to the top of Oats Peak. Ride back down to your car and drive toward the entrance for MDO, where you'll park at the trailhead for Hazard Canyon Road. Ride up and back. The next adventure (#21) is entirely dedicated to mountain biking Hazard Peak and Oats Peak. If you feel like spending a full day biking those two peaks and some more of the surrounding area, I recommend you take a look at that adventure.

Option 2: Double Summit to Sea Trail

The final option is what I call the Double Summit to Sea Trail. It first bags Valencia Peak, then Oats Peak, then follows Coon Creek Trail on its big loop back through the parking lot (with bathrooms), on to the Bluff Trail, and wraps back to the starting point. This option is approximately 9.5 miles and 1,900 feet of elevation gain. I like this one because it nabs you two peaks and is a little more straightforward than the Summit to Sea option. Bear in mind, however, this option will definitely have more traffic and bikers since Oats Peak Trail is one of the top mountain biking destinations in the park. But it still makes for an awesome day, and you will undoubtedly feel like you've accomplished something worthwhile — because you have!

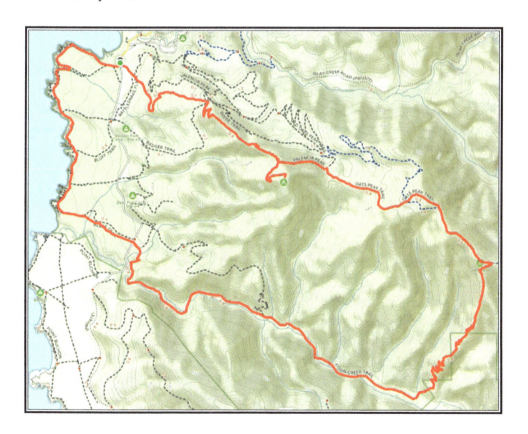

Mountain Biking in Montaña De Oro

One of the Top Mountain Biking Destinations on the Central Coast

What to Bring: mountain bike, hat, sunscreen, water, picnic, beers on ice
When to Go: Anytime
Duration/Distance: A few hours or extend to a full day

Directions to Start: From the 101, head west on Los Osos Valley Road (LOVR), which turns into Pecho Valley Road, and follow into Montaña de Oro State Park. Drive to the Hazard Peak Trailhead, which is on one of the final bends prior to reaching Spooner's Cove. There is parking in the dirt on both sides of the road.

I have a confession: I am not much of a mountain biker. In fact, real mountain bikers would call me an amateur, a rookie, a newbie, and perhaps a wuss. But I'll say this: Riding up the trails of Montaña de Oro (MDO) makes me want to be a mountain biker. MDO is one of the top two mountain biking destinations in SLO County, and Hazard Peak within MDO is probably the top ride people suggest. For those who like analogies, Hazard Peak is to SLO mountain biking as Bishop Peak is to SLO hiking. On a clear day, you can see waves rolling in along the entire 5-mile sandspit, Morro Bay, Morro Rock, and potentially all the way to the Piedras Blancas Light Station. The view is truly magnificent. Alternatively, on a much more common foggy day, you'll barely be able to see around the next blind corner, which is exciting in its own way.

In addition to Hazard Peak, below you'll find directions to extend the Hazard Peak ride via East Boundary Trail and to do the ride to Oats Peak. I hope you're ready for an **EPIC** day of riding!

Hazard Peak

If you've been mountain biking before, this trail should be very doable for you. If you're even more of a newbie than I am, this is probably not the first trail you should attempt, but the difficulty is really the length more than anything else, and you can always get off your bike and walk in the sections you find sketchy. So give it a go and build your confidence at your own pace.

Ascent to Hazard Peak

This ride can really be done any time of year, but you will cook on a hot day, because the trail is exposed most of the way. Check the weather before going and if it is supposed to be hot, try to get your ride in during the morning or late afternoon. The trail is also used by hikers and equestrians, so grab a bell from the box at the trailhead to keep everyone safe.

There are a few ways to do this ride:

Mountain Biking in Montaña De Oro

1) You can go to the peak and back, which is around six miles. If you're a total beginner, this is the best option.
2) You can continue down the back side of the peak and follow the trail all the way to Pecho Valley Road, then follow the paved road back to your car (around 8–9 miles).
3) You can do option 2 above and once you hit Pecho Valley Road, turn around and do the trail in reverse, making it an out and back. This option puts the ride at about 11 miles and is the recommended route.

The trail starts at a relatively low grade among the dunes. As you ascend, the grade will have steeper sections of consistent climbing that will have your heart pounding and the sweat pouring. You'll notice that the mountain biking trail wraps around the back side of the peak to get to the top, whereas the hiking trail allows hikers to approach from the front. Once at the peak, enjoy the view and have a snack or a picnic and decide what to do next. Go back the way you came (option 1), continue on to the road and loop back on the paved road (option 2), or make it an out and back (option 3). Base your decision on your energy level and riding confidence.

East Boundary Trail

Many riders like to add the East Boundary Trail to their ride, which adds several extra miles of riding and definitely kicks up the skill requirement. This option has a few downhill parts, which novices may want to walk down. You can tack this on to any of the aforementioned routes/options to get several miles of additional riding.

To add the East Boundary Trail, head east from Hazard Peak and instead of following the trail north, connect to East Boundary Trail. You'll want to follow the trail clockwise. The trail will take you down to Islay Creek Road, which you can use for a quick minute to head west and connect to the Barranca Trail (follow the arrows in the top pic of the next page), which can be used to loop back up. Once back at the top, you either head back past Hazard Peak to your parking spot or do the other half of the ride to the north toward Pecho Valley Road.

Back side of Hazard which goes to Pecho Valley Road

Spent? If so, you may want to head over to Spooner's Cove, break out a few chairs and some cold ones, and enjoy the beach. Still have fuel in the tank? Boom! Time for the second leg of your mountain biking outing.

Oats Peak Option

The other great riding option in the area is Oats Peak, an 11-mile out and back. The trailhead for Oats Peak is just south of Spooner's Cove. No need to repark your car — it's a quick ride over from the trailhead for Hazard Peak. The ride is a very straightforward out and back. The trailhead is about 100 feet up from the bathrooms on the road to the campground that turns in from Pecho Valley Road.

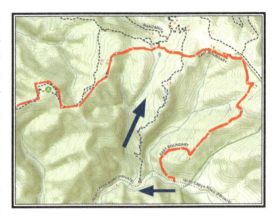

The ride to Oats Peak is a gradual 5.5-mile ascent that may just feel like it will never end. You will be mainly riding away from the ocean, encountering many twists and turns that allow for ocean views. You will be sharing the trail with hikers, so keep an eye out.

Once at the top, the hard work is over. Bask in the glory of the view you worked so hard to capture, then have a great time riding down. Again, you'll want to watch your speed down the hill since you're sharing the trail with hikers. Once at the bottom, your legs will be jelly

and you'll deserve some time at the beach. Head over, dip your feet, have a snack, and a few tasty beverages. You earned it!

Mountain Biking in Montaña De Oro

From Hazard Peak Trailhead parking, head down to the ocean on Hazard Reef Trail

Paso Robles Region
One of the Largest Wine Regions in the World Awaits

What to Bring: hat, sunscreen, water, picnic, designated driver
When to Go: Anytime
Duration/Distance: Multiple day trips

Directions to Start: 101 North to any loop option you choose

Pronounced Paso "row bulls" with no hint of its Spanish origin, and generally just called "Paso" by locals, many people are surprised to learn that Paso Robles has 40,000 vineyard acres — just under Napa's 43,000. Sonoma is the largest wine region in California with just over 60,000 acres. But unlike Napa and Sonoma, Paso is relatively less touristy, less snobby, and more down to earth.

Known for its heritage varietal Zinfandel, Cabernet Sauvignon, and Rhône-style wines, a trip to Paso takes you to the heart of one of the top wine regions in the world. What makes it even more amazing is that it has gone from only twenty wineries thirty years ago to around 300 wineries today, which is why some consider Paso the "Wild West" of wine regions in the U.S. If you're like me, you like wild. Paso was named the #6 place to visit in 2020 by *The New York Times*! See the article here: https://www.nytimes.com/interactive/2020/travel/places-to-visit.html.

A trip to Paso is not complete without wine, but it has way more to offer, and in this adventure, I'm going to whet your appetite for the rest of the region. Once you know Paso well, you can incorporate it into many of the other north county adventures in this book.

Paso Robles Region

When you head north from SLO on the 101 toward Paso, you travel up Cuesta Grade, aka "the Grade," a huge hill that takes you up over 1,000 feet in less than 10 minutes. Aside from being a speed trap on the way down and offering *killer views*, the Grade separates the mild climate of SLO with the harsher (relatively speaking) high desert of the Paso Robles region. In other words, north of the Grade, it is almost always hotter during the day and cooler at night than it is in SLO, so plan accordingly.

The busiest time of year in Paso is during harvest in October. This is a really fun time to visit, as many wineries offer grape stomping and other activities. Check online for "Harvest Weekend" so you don't miss it. One of the prettiest times of year to visit the region is late March through early May when everything is typically green and you'll feel like you're traveling through the hills of Ireland rather than the high desert of California.

The way I like to do this adventure is to start with a quick brekkie at home, do a hike of some sort while heading north, grab brunch or lunch, perhaps pop over to Tin City, spend a few hours driving through gorgeous wine country while wine tasting, and end the day in downtown Paso. Each portion of this trip can easily be extended for an entire day and you'll be forgiven if you never make it past the yard games at Barrelhouse in Tin City.

Check operating hours for any wineries you'd like to visit prior to starting out as the times may vary from what is listed within this adventure.

Paso Robles Region

Adventure Agenda	To Do
Breakfast	At home
Morning Adventure	Easy – East Cuesta Ridge or Atascadero Lake Easy/Medium - Three Bridges Oak Preserve Medium/Hard – Cerro Alto
Brunch/Lunch	The Fig at Courtney's House, pick from the wineries with food, or bring a picnic
Afternoon	Choose one of the five loops (Southwest, Midwest, Northwest, Northeast, Southeast), Tin City or head to downtown Paso
Sunset	Calcareous Winery
Dinner	Downtown Paso

Heading north, you have several good hiking options, each of which will be detailed below. Choose whichever fits your mood. Keep in mind that if you want to hike, you should do it on your way north, as Paso itself doesn't offer much in the way of hiking. The first trail you'll come to is at the very top of the Grade: Mount Lowe Trail, aka East Cuesta Ridge, a relatively flat 8-miler and is good for trail running. It's an out and back, so you can turn around whenever. Further north in Atascadero, you can do the easy 1.1-mile Atascadero Lake Preserve,

the moderate and dog-friendly Three Bridges Trail at 1.6 miles with extension option to 3.5 miles, or the most difficult hike of the options — Cerro Alto Trail Loop at 4.5 miles.

The Trail at the Top of the Grade (Mount Lowe Trail/East Cuesta)

The trailhead for Mount Lowe Trail is just over the hump of the Grade as you go up the hill on the east (right) side of the road. Almost no one knows the actual name of this hike, so many call it "the hike on the top of the Grade on the right" (catchy!) or "East Cuesta Ridge," which is not correct but makes sense since the other side of the 101 is where you find West Cuesta Ridge (another hiking option people love that you can try if you want to cross over the freeway traffic).

Poor marketing aside, East Cuesta (or whatever you want to call it) is a really pretty walk and is worth checking out any time. To get there, stay in the right lane and be ready to quickly pull off as soon as you crest the hill. Either park on the very short 50- to 100-foot dirt road that ends with a gate or in the parking area just next to the highway. Walk up the dirt road and jump the gate. This 8-mile out and back has a gradual ascent, some of the best views around (when it's not foggy), and, strangely, takes you into a pine forest! Who knew there were pine trees in SLO? This path makes for a solid trail run and is also regularly used by mountain bikers. The view is terrific!

East Cuesta parking area

Pine trees on East Cuesta

Atascadero Lake Park

If you want an easy option to stretch your legs, stop in Atascadero by taking the 41 West, and do the 1.3-mile walk around the Atascadero Lake Park, which is right next to the zoo. This is a great option if you have kids or a dog, or kids and a dog. Bonus, you get to hear the sounds of zoo animals.

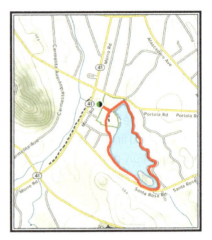

Three Bridges Oak Preserve

A little farther west off the 41 is the lovely Three Bridges Oak Preserve. Google the name, as the trailhead is well marked but tucked way back through a residential neighborhood with many turns to get to the trailhead. If you find the oaks in the Paso region as majestic as I do, you will really enjoy this hike! There is a 1.6-mile loop that takes you up and down. About halfway through the hike there is a spur that ascends another 400 feet or so over 0.8 miles. If you go up and down the spur, you basically double the length of the hike. This trail is pretty well used by locals and you'll likely see a decent amount of runners and people walking their dogs.

Cerro Alto Trail

Last on the list is Cerro Alto Trail Loop. This is one of the top trails in the region and offers a good workout with over 1,000 feet of elevation gain over 4.5 miles. Unless you like hot and dusty, try to do this hike outside of the peak heat in summer. During the other seasons or early mornings in the

summer, this is a great trail that offers *killer views* and really gets the blood flowing.

Atascadero

Now that you've worked up an appetite, you really can't go wrong having brunch at one of the local restaurants. In Atascadero, there are a bunch of good stops, including Sylvester's (burgers), AJ's Kitchen, Kochi Korean BBQ & Shabu Shabu, Wild Fields Brewhouse, and Street Side Ale House and Eatery. There are typically a few food trucks near downtown. Kuma, for example, crushes it just like their main restaurant in Los Osos. While in Atascadero, take a look at City Hall, which many consider the most beautiful building in SLO County. If you spend a moment on the big lawn listening to the fountains and looking at the gorgeous architecture, you will surprise yourself by temporarily thinking you're somewhere in Europe. Atascadero has arguably the best blockbuster movie theater in the county with the Galaxy Colony Square 10.

Atascadero's City Hall

Templeton

If you head a few minutes up the road, you can eat in Templeton at the Fig at Courtney's House, an adorable Victorian which feels like you've been invited to a good friend's house. McPhee's Grill and Pier 46 Seafood Market are two other great options. If you do this adventure on a Saturday, bonus, because you can walk out of Fig and across the street to the town square's Templeton Farmers' Market, a great spot to grab picnic fixins or simply bread, cheese, and a few pieces of fruit for afternoon snacks. If you need a coffee fix, head a few streets away to Spearhead Coffee.

Templeton Farmer's Market

Paso Wineries

You'd need weeks to properly visit every winery and back road in the Paso Robles region, so the best thing to do is explore just a few that are grouped together, drink responsibly, and come back to check out more on a future trip. You can break the wine areas into Paso west of the 101 and Paso east of the 101. I further break up these sections into several loops so you can keep your driving to a minimum while still hitting the best spots. West of the 101, I suggest a Paso "Southwest loop,"

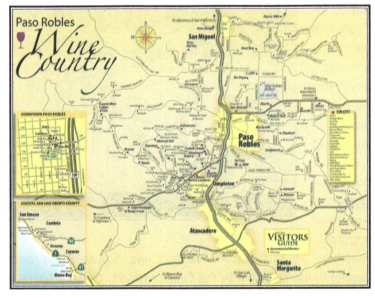

"Midwest loop," and "Northwest loop." East of the 101, I suggest a Paso "Northeast loop" and a "Southeast loop." There is also a section for the constantly growing, must-see area of Tin City. Follow any of these sections, then make your way to downtown Paso to finish your day.

While you'll be tempted to hit many of the wineries, it's best to visit only three to four wineries in a day if you plan to do a full tasting at each of them.

Use the map above or go to:
https://www.slovisitorsguide.com/paso-robles-wine-tasting-map/
Before we begin our wine tasting tour de force, I want to pause for a safety note. Since a lot of the offerings here center around drinking, if you don't have a designated driver, remember that whoever is driving should have no more than two tastings. If that seems impossible, you are highly encouraged to work with a company such as Uncorked Wine Tours (which even allows kids) or one of several other highly rated tour companies that will do the driving for you and typically get you behind-the-scenes tours at many wineries. No one wants to be on the road with intoxicated drivers, so please drink responsibly and we'll all make it home safe. On to the fun!

Paso Southwest Loop

There are so many excellent wineries on the 46 West, you can hit more than a dozen within five minutes of leaving the 101 and be in wine-tasting paradise.

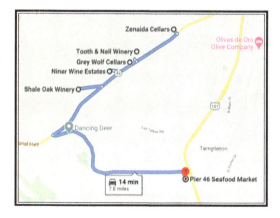

Head west on Highway 46 from the 101. Across from the J Dusi Wines (which is great), you can take Arbor Road north of the 46 and hit both Fratelli Perata (small family farm with unique Tuscan-style reds ... only club sales) and Austin Hope, or make your first stop Zenaida Cellars, which has incredible wine and a reasonably priced tasting. They are also one of the few wineries that has lodging, so consider that as part of a great multi-day trip. Peachy Canyon is across the street and has some great Zinfandels.

Continuing west on 46, you will pass Tooth & Nail Winery, which is a castle with a real moat (no alligators, though). If you have kids in tow, they will probably love this spot. Even the art, the labels of the wine bottles, and the employees are fashioned in the Gothic tradition. If you or your kids are goth, this will be a dream come true. If you are without kids, and goth doesn't mean anything to you, but you like castles, make a stop. Otherwise, continue west.

If it's Thursday through Monday, you definitely want to stop in at the unique Barton Family Wines/Gray Wolf Cellars/Krobar/Barton's Kitchen. You may feel like you are heading to someone's house. but don't let looks fool you. This friendly and unassuming little spot has something for everyone: one of the best winery restaurants in Paso, two unique wine tasting experiences, and a craft distillery (open Fri–Sun). Keep an eye out for the sign that points to the "Kitchen Window" — that is where you go to order food from Barton's Kitchen (open Thu–Mon 11:30am–4:30pm). Around back is Krobar, where the gin, whiskey, and rum make for great gifts. I'll admit that I passed this place at least a dozen times before I finally gave it a try and realized what I had been missing. Best to go Friday through Sunday if you want to try everything. However, the wines alone are excellent and worth the stop any day of the week.

Tasting room at Grey Wolf

Sextant, next door, is a local favorite. Then, as you continue west, look to your right. Notice the gigantic heart made of trees in the hill? This is Heart Hill, part of the next winery worth checking out: Niner Wine Estates. They have a gorgeous and vast tasting room and great wines; but even without them, I would still visit to support a winery that has done so much to push sustainability. They have solar panels that supply all their required energy, and then some. The facility is LEED Certified (Leader in Energy and Environmental Design) and built to responsibly use both water and energy. Additionally, this is the first winery in Paso Robles to be granted Sustainability in Practice (SIP) Certification, which means they farm sustainably and follow the 3 P's of sustainability: People, Planet, and Prosperity. Impressive, right?

A few blocks west, you'll jut right on Oakdale Road. Here, you'll find Shale Oak Winery (on your left). Similar to Niner, this winery was founded with the goal of making great wine without harming the environment. While their wine may not knock your socks off, this is a lovely stop, especially when they have live music. Across the street is Red Soles, which is highly recommended.

You now have two options for your route: 1) Call it a day, loop south on Vineyard Drive and head to Pier 46 Market or J&R Natural Meats to grab some grub to take home and grill, or 2) loop north for a pretty drive previewing the Midwest loop and make your way into downtown Paso.

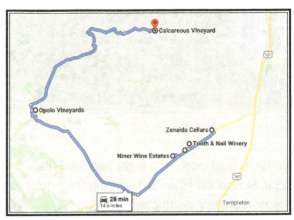

Assuming you want to do option 2 and take the scenic route and end in downtown Paso, continue west on Oakdale until you get to Vineyard Drive. Now go right.

You'll pass about a dozen wineries, then you'll come to Peachy Canyon Road and take a right. Follow this gorgeous, windy road for a few miles until you reach Michael Gill Cellars, which many insist have the best Syrah in the region. The tasting room is only open from 11 a.m.–5 p.m. Friday through Sunday or by appointment.

You might think you have already had an epic day, but want to make it even **EPIC**er? Calcareous Vineyard is like the grand finale of a fireworks display ... just when you think you've seen it all, the sky fills with explosions of wine and it covers the land below. With its sweeping vista over the Paso region, the views from this winery are magnificent. The only other winery that rivals this is Daou (Midwest loop). But unlike Daou, Calcareous is approachable and modest. For a great date — or if friends, parents, and/or kids are in town —consider coming back in the future to do a wine tour, wine and lunch pairing (on weekends), or the Hilltop Tasting Experience. Check their website for times and reservation details: https://www.calcareous.com/Visit/Tasting-Room

That brings an end to the Southwest Loop. Exhausted? Me too. Drunk? Catch an Uber. Head east a few minutes to downtown Paso Robles. Skip to the section on the downtown area to see what to do there.

Paso Midwest Loop

Start this loop following Vineyard Drive west of Highway 101. This loop picks up where the Southwest loop left off.

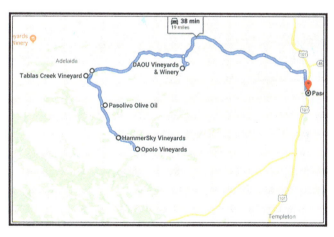

Your first stop will be Opolo Vineyards. This SIP Certified winery is one of the premier and best-known brands in the Paso region. Open from 10 a.m.–5 p.m. daily, you can get a wine tasting for $15 and add a cheese pairing for an additional $10. This makes a great first or second stop since they serve up really delicious wood-fired pizza daily from 10 a.m.–4 p.m.

Next up is HammerSky (11am–5pm daily) on your left, which offers Bordeaux-centric estate wines. This lovely spot offers gorgeous views and small-batch wines. Tastings are a little pricey at $20, but the price is waived with the purchase of two bottles. They have cheese and charcuterie available and you can reserve a sunset tasting on their website here: https://www.hammersky.com/tasting-reservations

Take a break from wine tasting with a visit to Pasolivo (11am–5pm). They also have a downtown location, but I prefer the ranch where they produce their olive oil. Tastings are $5 each and you can ask for a tour of the olive press.

Continue north a few hundred feet on Vineyard and go left on Adelaida Road to Tablas Creek Vineyard (10am–5pm) on your left. Tasting charge is $15 each but waived with the purchase of a bottle. This organic and sustainable winery has the bonus of a roaming herd of alpacas. If you have never seen alpacas, they are a cuter, smaller version of a llama, and in the event you ever want a cozy blanket, they offer some of the most comfortable fibers available. And these alpacas aren't just cute … they're working to guard the flock of sheep, who, in turn, have a job … to eat any non-vines and stomp/mulch the soil. But I digress. Back to the wine. This winery brought Rhone varietal grapes to the region. Consider booking their daily vineyard tour, which runs 45 minutes and departs at 10:30 a.m. and 2 p.m. at $15 per person. Reservations can be made here: https://tablascreek.com/visiting

Backtrack 100 feet toward Vineyard Drive, but follow Adelaida Road. Your next stop is the stately Halter Ranch Winery (M–Th 11am–5pm, Fri–Sun 10am–5pm) on the left. This is a very cool space. Tasting fee of $20, but waived with a two-bottle purchase. They have a seasonal food and wine pairing available Wednesday through Sunday from 11:30 a.m. to 3:30 p.m. Make sure you check out the caves, where a lot of their processing is done. Halter also offers a great two-hour Excursion Tour every day at 10 a.m. and a Vineyard Horseback Tour. Book on their website at https://www.halterranch.com/experience/vineyard-tours.

I'm a little conflicted about this last option, but read on and decide if it's for you. Daou Vineyards has one of the top two views (the other being Calcareous) in the region. The wines are very good. The seating both inside and outside offers stunning, sweeping views for miles in all directions. You will feel like you are on top of the world. This place is pretty highfalutin and makes no apologies. On weekends you will likely need to have a reservation since they get booked up early and routinely turn away walk-ins. Reservations or not, tastings are an astronomical $40 but waived if you buy three bottles! That'll keep the riffraff out! Are you hoity-toity or are you low-key? As Socrates said, "Know thyself." Depending on your answer, you'll love or hate this place.

The never-ending view from Daou

Continue east on Adelaida Road and you'll drop right into downtown Paso. Again, skip to the section on the downtown area to see what to do there.

Paso Robles Region

Paso Northwest Loop
We'll do this loop counterclockwise so you'll end in downtown. Start this loop following San Marcos Road west of Highway 101.

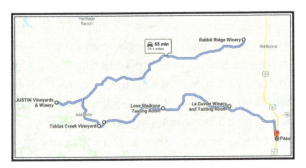

You will quickly get to Rabbit Ridge on your right (Fri – Sun 11am–4pm and, in winter, Sat–Sun 11am–4pm). This is a fun little family-run Mediterranean-style winery.

Follow San Marcos Road to where the road splits right to Nacimeinto Lake and follow the left fork on Chimney Rock Road. Detour alert: If you want some exercise before you wet your whistle, go to Lake Nacimiento where you can rent boats, paddle boards, or kayaks and enjoy the lake. Or head out on a hike next to the lake.

Justin is one of the best-known vineyards in the area and produces consistently solid wines. Locals may never forgive management for chopping down oaks to make way for vines, but those who don't know the history show up in droves to taste ($35 each) their great wines. They have a good cave tour with tasting. You can also enjoy their wine at their new and very hip downtown Paso location.

Backtrack to Adelaida Road and go south (right). Check out Tablas Creek Vineyard, then wrap around the corner to the left to taste at Halter Ranch Vineyard. With tasty SIP Certified Bordeaux-style and Rhone-style wines, Halter Ranch is a must stop as it is one of the most lovely and inviting vineyards in Paso. It's getting more visitor-friendly by the day (some might say commercialized) and they are installing a light rail soon. Fun fact: This is where Ronald Reagan announced he was running for his second presidential term.

Follow Adelaida Road to the Adelaida Winery, then cross the street to Lone Madrone Tasting Room. Continue east, making a stop at Le Cuvier before dropping into downtown Paso Robles at 24th Street. Skip to the section on the downtown area to see what to do there.

Paso Northeast Loop

If you're planning to see a show at Vina Robles Amphitheatre or if you have kids who regularly

go to the Ravine Waterpark, you can check off the wineries below over time. Otherwise, this small loop packs in a lot of great wineries in a very short distance.

Take the 46 East from the 101 and stop in at EOS (11am–5pm daily), a highly regarded winery in a nice location that makes for a good starting point for your loop. **SLOcals Only Pro Tip:** If it's summer and you have kids who can be on their own, drop them off at the Ravine Water Park across the street, then come over for some relaxing adult time.

Next up is Mitchella Vineyard and Winery (11am–4:30pm Th–Mon). This relatively hidden, family-owned spot is off most tourists' radars and offers a nice contrast to some of the larger wineries trying so hard to wow you with over-the-top extravagance. A cheese pairing is included with the tasting fee, which is $15 for one or $20 if shared for two. Buy two bottles to get the tasting waived. Their wines are small-batch, so you can only buy them on site or at a few local shops.

Vina Robles is your next destination. From its first six vineyards planted back in 1996, Vina Robles now boasts many more vineyards, a 14,000-square-foot hospitality center, and the Vina Robles Amphitheatre, which is easily the best location for an outdoor event in the region. Tastings (10am–5pm daily) are $15 but waived if you buy a bottle. They also have a wine and cheese pairing daily from 11 a.m. to 3 p.m. for $30. **SLOcals Only Pro Tip:** If you are a regular at the amphitheater and you like Vina Robles' wine, if you join the Vina Robles Wine Club, you get priority access to purchase tickets for a majority of the concerts, and before the shows starts, you are given access to their club for free wine tasting.

Next on our loop is Eberle, a top-rated winery by locals and critics alike. (Open 10am–6pm Apr–Oct; 10am–5pm Nov–Mar.) Eberle released its first wine in 1979, making it one of the more established wineries in the region. With free cave tours, an outside picnic deck, bocce ball and cornhole, this winery offers a lot to do. Did I mention that tastings are free? Well, I have now. If you're keeping track, that means Eberle offers the best deal in town.

Bianchi Winery (Th–Mon 10am–5pm) has put a lot of thought into making wine tasting an immersive experience. You are highly encouraged to bring a picnic, play yard games, feed the koi fish, and generally linger for a while. With complimentary tastings, this is a great stop on any tour in the region.

Penman Springs (Th–Mon 11am–5pm) is a family-owned artisan winery offering complimentary tastings with a purchase. This is a great little winery with many estate-grown varieties, including Cabernet Sauvignon, Muscat Blanc, Merlot, Petite Sirah, and Petit Verdot.

If you're not quite ready to head to dinner, here's a brief detour that'll make your day **EPIC**: Check out River Oaks Hot Springs Spa (9am–9pm daily) at 800 Clubhouse Drive, which offers all your normal spa services, as well as private one-hour soaks in a mineral spa for $16 Monday through Thursday and $22 Friday through Sunday. Reserve ahead of time.

Now skip to the section on downtown Paso and go get some great food to close out your day.

Paso Southeast Loop

This is the only loop that doesn't wrap up in downtown Paso, so you'll have different options for how to finish up your day, which I'll get to a bit later. But first, let's enjoy some great wine! Put Sculpterra in your GPS and we'll start there.

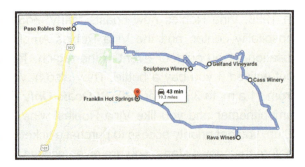

Sculpterra (10am–5pm daily) is one of the most unique wineries you can visit in the region. With lovely grounds that include valuable sculptures and a large and varied wine-tasting area, this fun spot is definitely worth a stop and a stroll.

Gelfand, which is just past Sculpterra, is a very small winery that puts out some very good wines. To taste, you'll need to arrange ahead of time by calling (805) 239-5808 or e-mailing len@gelfandvineyards.com.

Next on your tour is Cass Winery (11am–5pm daily), where you can wine taste, eat at their café, or do one of the activities they offer through their Camp Cass, which includes things such as olive-oil pressing, beekeeping, a race around their 145-acre winery, and a photo scavenger hunt. The winery also has accommodations available and some really fun events (i.e., a sunset seafood boil with live music). Check their website (https://www.casswines.com/) so you can plan around any event that speaks to you.

Continue south on Geneseo Road and take Creston Road west (back toward the 101). Go left (south) on Showdown Lane to Rava Winery (11am–5pm). This is one of the best stops if you like sparkling wines. A tasting for regular (still) wine is $15 and $20 for sparkling, and the fee is waived with a two-bottle purchase. Custom cheese and charcuterie plates are available. But wait, what would make cheese and wine even better? Enjoying said cheese and wine by a lake. They have one of those, too.

Making sparkling wine is much harder than you may think. From their website: "Rava Wines is the first winery in Paso Robles to focus on sparkling wines crafted using the time-honored méthode champenoise technique. The cuvée, or base wine, is made from grapes strategically harvested at slightly earlier stages of ripeness to capture the natural acidity and phenolic complexity. The cuvée goes through primary fermentation in a combination of neutral French barrels and stainless-steel tanks. The cuvée, along with a mixture of sugar, yeast and nutrients, are bottled for the secondary fermentation where it's aged en tirage and benefits from contact with the lees. The wine is then riddled and disgorged using state-of-the-art equipment in the Rava cellar. Finally, a small dosage is added before the sparkling wine is sealed." Rava recently opened a 17,000-square-foot event center, so check their site https://ravawines.com/concert-schedule/ for upcoming events.

You now have a few options for finishing up your day. If you want to keep going west on Creston Road, you'll drive right past the Franklin Hot Springs at 3015 Creston Road. (8am–10pm, $7 entrance fee per person.) Let me be the first to warn you: This is not some posh, resort-style, fancy hot spring with a bunch of robe-wearing, daquiri-drinking, hoity-toity aristocrats. This is a rustic, geothermal lake with no frills, and some might say it's barely developed. They might even say it's run-down. Whatever you call it, the water will rejuvenate you and the price is tough to beat, so check it out or swing back by in the future.

Assuming you're hungry and assuming you've never been to Creston before, I'm going to give you two reasons to go: The Longbranch Saloon (Wed–Sat 11am–8:30pm; Sun 11am–6:30pm) and the Loading Chute Restaurant & Barn (Mon–Sat 11am–9pm; Sun 9am). Both locations will make you feel as if you've gone back in time about 100 years and serve you so much food you'll feel like you won't need to eat for another 100 years. Roll yourself out of the restaurant after dinner and head up to the 41, then follow it west to the 101 as you make your way home.

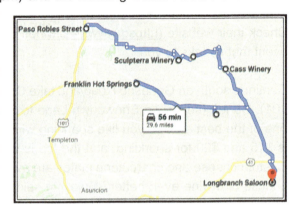

Downtown Paso

Downtown Paso has tons of wine tasting, top-notch restaurants, fun shops, and is great for strolling. The heart of the city is just north of the town square, which is called Downtown City Park. You could bypass everything else in this chapter and just head downtown and you'd have a great day. When I took a friend to eat in Paso for the first time, she couldn't hide her anger that I never told her how good the food is here. Well, the cat's out of the bag. The food is great. Also, there's wineries, breweries, and distilleries popping up everywhere. Even if you did a wine tasting tour in downtown, you wouldn't be able to go to all the spots in one day. Okay, maybe you could, but you wouldn't be able to walk by the end. Below is a map from the Paso Wine Stroll held in 2019.

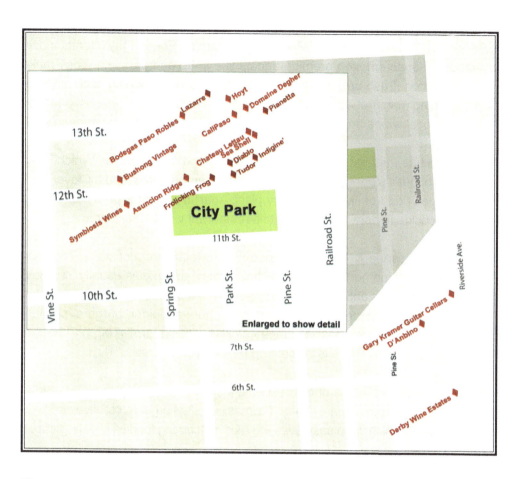

Since so many of the loop adventures end in Paso, here is a little information on some of the restaurants you may want to try:

Fish Gaucho is a self-proclaimed hip spot for Mexican food. They've got some of the most gourmet Mexican food in the county, a solid selection of margarita options, and fresh-made chips with multiple dipping sauces.

Il Cortile has been around for more than 10 years and has a huge following. You'll likely need to make a reservation well in advance to get a spot here. This Italian restaurant is among the top choices in town. I hate to be predictable, but try the pasta.

Jeffry's Wine Country BBQ opened in 2018 and has quickly established itself as a local favorite. Framing itself as "Wine Country Comfort Food," they offer their own dry-rubbed, house-smoked premium meats like tri-tip and pork loin. They make their own bacon, fresh bread, and sauces from scratch; they have a selection of award-winning mac n' cheese and paella; they have vegetarian options; and they have eight local wines and eight craft beers on tap. Is your mouth watering yet?

La Cosecha has the best South American food in the county by far. Which is not saying much, but it's good nonetheless. Ceviche, empanadas, and a Clover Club South cocktail (kind of like a raspberry pisco sour) make for a pretty darn good meal. The cocktails here alone make this restaurant worth checking out.

The Hatch Rotisserie & Bar offers wood-fired cuisine and cocktails. The food comes out on cutting boards in a really fun display, and meals usually include a good combo of mains and vegetables. Start with beets, brussels sprouts, roasted carrots, hot-skillet cornbread, then move on to pork shoulder, burgers, salmon, shrimp and grits, or their half rotisserie chicken with buttermilk dip and house-fermented hot sauce. There is something for everyone here.

Thomas Hill Organics is one of the best eateries in Paso. Just north of 13th Street directly north of the town square center, Thomas Hill offers organic, creative, delicious gourmet options which will please even the most discerning foodies in your group.

Don't leave downtown without doing a stroll around the city park and stopping in at the General Store Paso Robles, which sits on the northern side of the square. This shop is super fun, has tons of local items, and is the place to go if you want to bring home a great gift. If you like the people you live or work with, you should stop in at Brown Butter Cookies and grab a few bags. When you share these little morsels of buttery deliciousness, you are guaranteed to receive love and affection.

Finally, while wineries get all the attention, there are some great breweries in Paso. Silva Brewing on the southern side of town was started by the brewmaster from Green Flash Brewing Company in San Diego, which has been rated among the nation's Top 50 craft breweries by RateBeer.com. Other spots to check out in downtown include Toro Creek Brewing Company, Earth and Fire Brewing Company, Santa Maria Brewing Co., and California Coast Brewing Company.

It's not downtown, but the most well-known brewery in the Central Coast is just east of the 101. Firestone Walker Brewing Company has grown from a small local brewery into one of the top-selling craft breweries in the nation. Every time you visit, there is something new. These days you can find a taproom with a full restaurant, go on brewery tours, and a must-visit is their beer emporium located a few blocks south of the taproom. The emporium is a beer lover's dream come true and the place to go if you want to stock up on large quantities of Firestone Beer.

Tin City
Tin City demands its own section, as this industrial area spanning a few streets and dozens of businesses has grown from nothing into a microcosm of the entire Paso region and is now a destination in its own right. Sure, you can "pop by" for an hour or two, but with expanding food offerings, more than a dozen tasting rooms, great ice cream, and the most family-friendly brewery in the county, you will likely stay much longer. Tin City should be on even the shortest Paso Robles itinerary, and on a nice, sunny day, you'll be hard-pressed to find a reason why you'd want to go anywhere else. Check out the map below from locally run Toast Tours, which offers all types of great tours of the region.

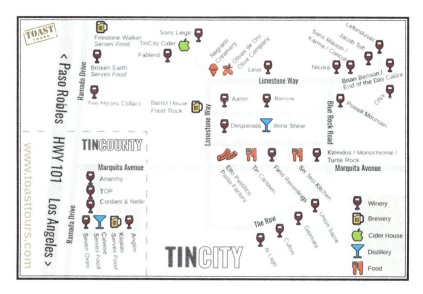

Let's start with Barrel House brewery since it has what I consider the most welcoming beer garden for hundreds of miles. With all types of lawn games, a fun water feature, free pretzels, great beers, rotating food trucks, occasional live music, and lots of space for kids to run around, this is the type of business where you go and think, "Nailed it!" Their open inside and outside floorplan takes advantage of California's nearly always perfect weather and reminds you why people love to live in this state.

If beer isn't your thing, take a stroll over to Tin City Cider, which has concoctions such as the tropical, pineapple-infused Parrothead; the barrel-aged bourbon Templetucky, which has a touch of blood orange; Polly Dolly, which has rose and watermelon notes; and the Original Dry Hopper Cider, which has a green apple, citrus, champagne thing going on. The point is, if you like cider, you'll like Tin City Cider.

With more than a dozen wineries in Tin City, you could spend the better part of the day trying all of them. At a minimum, you should check out Giornatta and Turtle Rock, both of which are highly rated by critics and locals.

Finally, for food options, check out Tin Canteen for pizza and pasta if you want a sit-down restaurant. Otherwise, go to Etto, which has a great selection of imported Italian goods and fresh homemade pastas to either take home or make a picnic.

Finally, no trip to Tin City is complete without a visit to Negranti Creamery. With 16 handcrafted flavors of both sheep's milk and cow's milk ice cream, ice cream sandwiches, and ice cream pies, this spot is a delight.

Distillery Tour

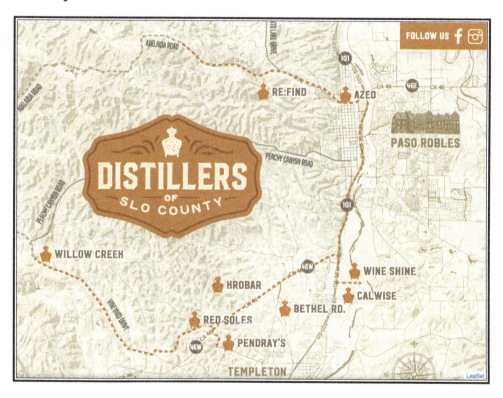

First it was wineries, then craft breweries, and now, distilleries are popping up all over the county. If you like gin, grappa, vodka, or whiskey, this will be a fun day for you. You can add these distillers to any of the wine tasting loops above, or, to avoid mixing, do a distillery day trip. Some of these distillers are at great wineries (which is helpful in the event people in your party don't want liquor), and some have food available. While all of the spots I mention are open during the weekend, hours vary, and only some open during the rest of the week. Check out this site for more info: http://www.pasoroblesdistillerytrail.com/

Starting at Re:Find and going clockwise, here's what you can find at each location:

Re:Find (daily 11am–5pm): vodka, gin, rye whiskey, bourbon, vermouth
Azeo (weekends Noon–4pm): cider, vodka, brandy, rum, coffee liqueur
Wine Shine (Th–Sun from 1pm): Many flavors of Brandy, Manhattan Project
Calwise (Th–Fr 4–9pm; Sat Noon–9pm; Sun Noon–6pm): rum, gin, whiskey, vodka, brandy, liqueuers, food and cocktails
Bethel Rd (Th–Mon Noon–6pm): grappa, aged brandy, gin
Pendrays (Th–Mon 11–4): brandy, grappa, liqueurs
Krobar at the back of Gray Wolf Winery (Th–Mon 11am-5:30pm): gin, brandy, rye whiskey, bourbon, bitter liqueur
Red Soles (11am–4pm): brandy
Willow Creek (Sat–Sun 11am–4pm): grappa, fruit brandy

After your day at Paso's distilleries, have your designated driver head back to SLO, and, assuming you are still coherent, check out the options in town. The tasting room at Rod & Hammer's, which is attached to the Rock at SLO Brew, is the whiskey tasting room of your dreams and is open late. If you are a fan of brandy, head to Autry Cellars.

Whew! What a day/week/month. You are now an expert of wines, beers, and spirits. You'll need to come back every six months just to keep up with all the new spots as they open. For now, give your liver a well-deserved rest, and perhaps consider a cleanse.

Wildflowers off 58

Beautiful Wildflowers, a Roller Coaster Road, and an Old West Feel

What to Bring: hat, sunscreen, water, picnic, chairs, small mobile picnic table or blanket, nice camera and tripod, walking/hiking shoes, kayak
When to Go: during "super bloom" ~Feb–May
Duration/Distance: 3 hours to all day

Directions to Start: 101 North to Santa Margarita, east through town to Highway 58, follow the 58 to Shell Creek Road

While this drive is an adventure any time of year, an amazing phenomenon occurs in SLO County from around February until May: a super bloom with wildflowers everywhere. Nowhere is this display more evident and abundant than off one of the windiest and most nausea-inducing roads you've ever traveled: Highway 58. I like to start this trip really early before sunrise when the sky is still changing colors and the oaks seem even more majestic than usual. Evening is also great. Middle of the day can be scorching hot in the summer, but not too bad the rest of the year.

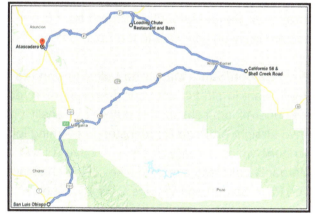

If you're planning on taking photos, the morning or evening is when you'll get the best light. While I'm going to assume you will do this trip during the wildflower bloom, you should really consider doing this adventure a few different times during the year. You'll find that the contrasting seasons make for beautiful and varied settings, and if you happen to be lucky enough to hit upon a foggy day,

Wildflowers off 58

you will feel transported to another world. Prior to setting off on this trip, have your directions pretty dialed in since cell service is spotty or nonexistent.

Start by traveling north of SLO on Highway 101 "up the grade." After reaching the top of the Grade, Santa Margarita is only a few miles away. Exit the 101 and head east through this very cool little town. Don't blink or you'll miss it. Some of the best stops in town are the rustic wood shop; the antique store; Range, which is one of the Top 10 dinner places in SLO County; Ancient Peaks, a great place to wine taste; and definitely stop at the Caliwala Food Market for your picnic fixings. After passing the exorbitantly priced gas station on the right look for the next main turn, head right over the train tracks. After a few hundred feet, the road curves sharply to the left — this is typically where you can see a sign telling you if the Pozo Saloon is open. Follow the road for a few miles as it curves along and keep your eyes peeled for where you turn left to stay on Highway 58. I repeat, you have to turn left, and the turn is really easy to miss. If you've been driving away from Santa Margarita for more than five minutes and haven't turned left, you are likely on your way to the Pozo Saloon. Which brings us to a fun detour.

Pozo Saloon/Santa Margarita Lake/Rinconada Trail
If you want to stretch out your day or if you're doing this adventure outside of the super-bloom season, this detour can easily become your adventure. Simply drive straight on Pozo Road instead of turning left for Highway 58. Besides the scenery, which is really pretty, you have a few good activity choices: 1) Santa Margarita Lake and a related hike, 2) the challenging RInconada Trail, and/or 3) The Pozo Saloon and Vintage Cowboy Winery.

Santa Margarita Lake
Coming from Santa Margarita on Pozo Road, you will first encounter the road to Santa Margarita Lake. Take a left (north), you will likely need to pay a $10 entry fee for the lake. Park near the Gray Pine campground and do the 4.4 mile Gray Pine Trail. If you have a

kayak, you can kayak for miles in this relatively quiet but peaceful lake. There is also camping which you can reserve through the county website at slocountyparks.com, and if you want to kick your camping up a few notches on the adventure scale, you can reserve a spot here and do a kayak camping trip.

Rinconada Trail

After the lake — or if you've skipped the lake and you are heading east away from Santa Margarita — consider doing the Rinconada Trail if you want a butt-kicker of a hike, a 4.7-mile loop (give yourself 2 to 2.5 hours and bring lots of water). This hike begins approximately 9.5 miles past where Highway 58 splits off to the left. Look for a sign for the turnoff, then follow it on a very short, unpaved road that dead-ends at the trailhead. The trails starts on the east side of the parking lot. There is a sign at the trailhead showing the hike.

Kayak camping at Santa Margarita Lake

Rocky top of Rinconada Trail

Wildflowers off 58

Pozo Saloon/Vintage Cowboy Winery
Continuing east for another 10 to 15 minutes, you come to the Pozo Saloon, a very cool Old West-style bar. Note it is usually only open on weekends. Next door is Vintage Cowboy Winery, which is well worth a stop.

Shell Creek Road – Wildflower Bloom
Assuming you stayed the course and didn't do the detour to Santa Margarita Lake, you have now gone left to stay on Highway 58. You are about to experience several miles of ridiculously windy roads, curvaceous some might even call them, because they're curvy yet beautiful. One turn in particular gets a special shout-out since it is more than 180 degrees! After this, there are a few more twists, a few more shouts (Chubby Checker anyone?) then the road straightens out and you can get back to a normal speed.

Continue on your merry way for about twenty minutes until you get to Shell Creek Road, which may or may not have a sign, and you will probably not have cell service. Keep an eye out for a nice straight stretch with flat land around (as opposed to the hills you've been seeing), a road that goes perpendicular off to the left, a windmill somewhat tucked behind trees just off of Shell Creek Road, and if you miss the turn, you will pass over a very low bridge and will need to turn around.

Drive north on Shell Creek Road for five minutes or so as you scout out the perfect spot for your picnic or photo shoot. Park wherever you like. Many people choose to picnic in the shade under one of the large oaks. Get out and explore to find the perfect picture. If you're here during wildflower season, you should see them everywhere.

Try not to trample the flowers so others can enjoy. Look for the few trails that run parallel to Shell Creek Road if you'd like to meander through the flowers.

Wildflowers off 58

Wildflowers off 58

Carrizo Plain National Monument

If you want to make this a huge day, continue heading east another 30 to 45 minutes from Shell Creek Road to the Carrizo Plain National Monument. It may feel like you are going to the middle of nowhere, which is true. Sound adventurous? You bet!

Your journey will take you past one of the largest solar projects in the world (Topaz Solar Farms), a sight unto itself considering it takes up as much, if not more, space than the city of San Luis Obispo and consists of a mind-boggling 8 million solar panels. This is what it looks like to power 150,000 homes with solar panels. If you're wondering, the power from the plant is sent to PG&E and is then distributed to PG&E customers. If you are a PG&E customer in SLO, you can feel good knowing that part of your power is produced locally in our county and is likely coming from this solar project, as are the related property taxes! You can thank your local politicians for making this happen.

Enough about solar, though. The Carrizo Plain National Monument keeps some wacky hours, so check it out before you go there (https://www.blm.gov/programs/national-conservation-lands/california/carrizo-plain-national-monument). For instance, one of the monument's highlights is the Painted Rock, which you can see on a 1.4-mile self-guided tour from July 16–Feb. 28 or on a docent-led hike during the bird nesting season on Saturdays from the third Saturday in March to the last Saturday in May.

A trip to the Carrizo Plains will be most enjoyable during wildflower season because it is not too hot and there are wildflowers everywhere. Bonus: You can literally see the San Andreas Fault when you are out here, so perhaps look out for that beachfront property you want after California breaks away from the mainland.

After Shell Creek Road

If you are finished visiting the Carrizo Plain, or if you are skipping it because you don't want to tack on the extra hours for a visit, there are several other good options in the area. From Shell Creek Road and Highway 58, you can: 1) Check out the buffalo (that's right — buffalo!), 2) Go on a guided horseback ride, or 3) Eat like a cowboy/cowgirl, 4) Visit a hot spring.

For the buffalo, you have to be somewhat lucky with your timing as they are typically off Highway 58 on the north side, where they tend to walk through the hills or near the road. Don't go too close and don't go over the fence to look for them — these things are huge and dangerous and don't take kindly to people up in their business.

If horseback riding is for you, or even if you're a newbie, you'll really enjoy one of the tours offered by Central Coast Trailrides off of Donovan Road. You'll need to call ahead and make reservations (805-610-1306).

If you have a major appetite, you may want to head north on Donovan to the Loading Chute Restaurant and Barn in the tiny town of Creston. What the town lacks in size, they make up for in portions. Get ready for a large portion of food. Not large. Really large. A thick and juicy steak and fixins the way cowboys used to eat them. I usually split one meal with my wife and we can't finish.

Depending on how many of the options you included in your day, it's probably already been pretty **EPIC,** but here's one last option to make it **EPIC**er ... maybe.

Franklin Hot Springs
Since you are the adventurous type, I will do my best to set your expectations low for this option, and then you may be pleasantly surprised. I present you with the Franklin Hot Springs (3015 Creston Road), which is a hop, skip, jump, and algae-covered splash from Creston. Think of the nicest hot spring resort you've ever visited, then imagine what that place would look like after it had burned down during the apocalypse. Now, you have a good idea of what you're in for, and with this frame of mind, there is no doubt you will enjoy your end-of-the-world dip much more. Opening at 7a.m. daily and open until 10 p.m. Monday through Thursday and until midnight on Friday through Sunday, the entrance fee is $7 per adult.

Inner Child – Adventure for Kids of All Ages

24

A Choose Your Own Adventure That Is Highly Enjoyable for All

What to Bring: hat, sunscreen, water, walking shoes, towels
When to Go: Anytime
Duration/Distance: A few hours to a full day

Directions to Start: 101 South to San Luis Bay Drive exit, go straight onto Ontario Road

The SLO region is a veritable playground for kids of all ages. I regularly make the mistake of asking my young girls if they want to go for a hike. The answer is almost always "no." But when I ask with excitement in my voice if they want to go on an adventure, the answer is almost always an eager "yes!" To which I reply with enthusiasm that they need to grab some sturdy shoes and some layers, because on an adventure, anything can happen and you need to be prepared. See if this approach works for you when you set out for the kid-friendly destinations in this chapter. (While these selections are geared toward kids under 10, older kids will love many of them, too.)

Bob Jones Trail

Have a quick snack at home or in the car on the way to the Bob Jones Trail. Park at the lot at 7009 Ontario Road and cross over the road to the start of the path. This 2.3-mile walk is almost completely flat, paved, and is very bike- and stroller-friendly. This is a very popular walk for good reason: It's  beautiful, follows a gorgeous canyon, parallels a lovely creek, and ends at the ocean in Avila. You can stop halfway at the Woodstone Marketplace if you need a pit stop or some supplies. My preferred option is to make a brief detour at

Sycamore Mineral Springs Resort and buy a Doc Burnstein's ice cream sandwich from their gift shop, then enjoy it on their meticulously groomed grounds.

The trail ends at the intersection that leads to the town of Avila. Cross over diagonally, walk toward town, and then go right, where you will see the Central Coast Aquarium. There's also Avila Beach Park, a kid favorite.

Have a Doc's treat

The Bob Jones Trail

Inner Child – Adventure for Kids of All Ages

The perfectly placed park in Avila

Inner Child – Adventure for Kids of All Ages

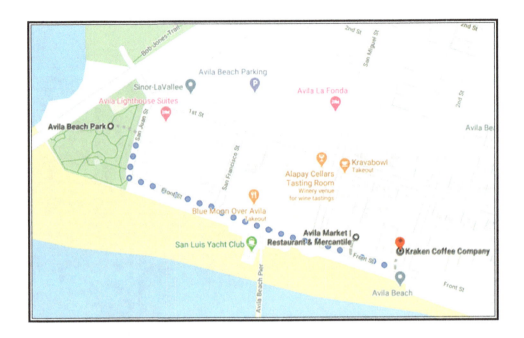

But before we go to the park, if it's morning, I like to head up to the boardwalk (the road parallel to the ocean) called Front Street and follow it to the Avila Market for delicious açaí, yogurt, and fruit bowls from Kravabowl. Buy a large bowl to go and share with your kids at the playground. If you haven't had your coffee fix, head a few shops down from the Avila Market to the Kraken Coffee Company, a great little coffee shop overlooking the ocean.

After you're finished at the playground, you can head down to the beach to explore, walk around Avila, go to the aquarium, grab a bite at one of the beachfront restaurants, or head back to your car. In the event you head back to your car, you may want to take a quick detour to Sycamore Mineral Springs Resort, which is detailed further below.

Surf and games at the pier in Avila

Avila Valley Barn

Once back to your car, drive south to Avila Beach Drive and hang a right to get to the Avila Valley Barn. This is a kid favorite and has produce, nuts, food, animals to see and pet out back, and you can even go for a hayride.

Inner Child – Adventure for Kids of All Ages

Hot Springs in Avila

Ready for a relaxing swim? You have two options within minutes of the Avila Valley Barn: Avila Hot Springs or Sycamore Mineral Springs Resort & Spa. Avila Hot Springs is more kid-friendly and less expensive, but also more crowded. It doubles as a campground with RV parking and is located right next to the 101. It has a big pool with a few slides, and a hot pool that is basically a kiddie pool hot spring. Kids really like this place, parents less so since the hot pool is so small and filled with kids. Get a discounted rate before noon.

The Sycamore Mineral Springs Resort & Spa is much more upscale. Make a note to come back sometime and stay, since all their rooms have a private hot tub on the patio. In the meantime, you can rent one of their hillside private hot tubs by the hour. It's usually no problem renting during the week, but you should call ahead for weekend use. Bring your own towels so you don't have to rent any. They have a gift shop with snacks and adult beverages you can take to your private hot tub.

Soak among the oaks at Sycamore Mineral Springs

When you arrive, park near the entrance to the gift shop, which is where you check in for the hot tubs. The gift shop is on the right just past the main reception area. Depending on how much time you have, you can add in a moderate or easy hike. For the moderate hike, take Sycamore Trail, which starts on the road just next to the main resort hotel entrance. This eventually turns to a dirt trail which leads to the top of the ridge and provides a *killer view* over all of Avila and the Pacific Ocean. For the easy hike, find the bridge that crosses over Avila Road and follow this bridge to the Bob Jones Trail. You may even want to bring a book along.

Starting Point for the Sycamore Trail

For the soak, note that you should arrive ten minutes early. Bring a towel (to save yourself renting one). Each hot tub is private, so bathing suits are optional. I usually bring a bag with a towel, a book or journal, snacks, and perhaps a cold beverage. Bringing outside snacks is frowned upon, as they request you buy from the check-in area where they have a great selection of wine, beer, and snacks. In the event you get a massage, you will have access to both their small spa facility that includes a locker room with shower, and their reception area, where there is hot tea, water, and usually fruit. Sitting on the patio out back is pretty.

Apples and Peacocks

After spending the morning in Avila, you might want to do a quick drive up See Canyon to grab some apples at the Gopher Glen Organic Apple Farm, then head  over to have some wine at See Canyon Vineyards, where your kids will be entertained by the dozens of peacocks roaming the grounds as you relax. Alternatively, as you head back to SLO on the 101, you may want to stop off to pick apples or produce at SLO Creek Farms at 6455 Monte Road.

Afternoon Activity

For your afternoon, what sounds best? A hike, something educational, crafting, or a fantastic park? For a hike, head to Islay Hill. For education, go to the San Luis Obispo Children's Museum. For crafting, head to Pipsticks. For a park, Sinsheimer Park is the best in town.

Islay Hill

Islay Hill is located off Orcutt Road east of Broad Street. I like to take Spanish Oaks Drive east of Orcutt Road, then follow to the end and go left on Sweet Bay Lane. Park near the cul-de-sac and follow the trailhead. This is a relatively easy trail (my 5-year-old can do it without help) but does have some decent elevation gain. The views of the coastline and Edna Valley wineries are great.

Inner Child – Adventure for Kids of All Ages

San Luis Obispo Children's Museum
The San Luis Obispo Children's Museum is located in downtown SLO and is great for kids around 6 and under. This is a hands-on science and discovery museum and will easily keep young children occupied for a few hours. Bonus:

Walk down to the creek before or after the museum and the kids will have a blast. Since you're in the area, you may want to stop in at Tom's Toys to reward your kids if they've behaved. Or take them over to Rocket Fizz, a really fun candy shop, or Doc Burnstein's, the most kid-friendly ice cream shop in town.

Pipsticks
Routinely referred to as "the sticker store," Pipsticks on Monterey Street has more stickers than you can shake a stick at. Additionally, they have fun things to color, craft, tape, and draw. If your child likes stickers or crafting, they will love this place.

Get crafty at Pipsticks

Sinsheimer Park
Sinsheimer Park is located just behind Sinsheimer Elementary School and was recently remodeled for close to $2 million, easily making it the best park in town. The park has slides, ropes, swings, a hill to slide down, and even a zip line! Bring a blanket to sit on in the grass while your kids expend all their energy.

Dinner Options

The thought of dinner with kids always makes me hesitate a little. How many times have I gone to a restaurant with my girls only to rush through the meal so I can get my ticking time bombs out of there before they go off? It really takes a lot of the fun out of eating out. Still, there's a few good family-friendly restaurants where I don't worry as much. In SLO, there's Village Host, Eureka Burger (which always has great beers on tap), and for a more upscale experience, the Madonna Inn, which is always a kid- pleaser. In Paso, BarrelHouse Brewery is mainly outdoors and very kid friendly. In Arroyo Grande, there's Klondike

Pizza, which has games and peanuts (kids can throw shells on the floor). Doc Burnstein's is just a few doors down.

To round out your day, consider heading to the Sunset Drive-In Theater which is extremely fun and offers a double feature; the first movie is usually kid-friendly and the second is usually meant for a slightly older audience when the kiddos have fallen asleep.

Other Options to Entertain Kids

While this chapter has many cool activities to bring out your inner child or cater to your little ones, it is by no means a complete representation of everything worth doing with kids in the region. For example, Big Creek in Paso is a really fun water park worth checking out in the summer. The Christmas chapter (adventure #37) has tons of events your kids will love. Watching the elephant seals in San Simeon mesmerizes kids for hours. And perhaps best of all, our many miles of beaches are endlessly entertaining.

Sunset in Pismo Beach

Ontario Ridge Trail (Sycamore Crest) to Pirate's Cave and Pirate's Cove

25

Moderate to Difficult Hike Loop with Ocean Reward

What to Bring: hat, sunscreen, water, a good book, snacks, swimsuit (optional)
When to Go: Anytime
Duration/Distance: 5+ miles with optional biking extension

Directions to Start: Driving south on the 101 from SLO, get off at Avila Beach Drive and go straight through the intersection on Shell Beach Road, go right on El Portal Drive, and park in the neighborhood. Trailhead is just north of El Portal on the left.

If you're looking for a tough hike with gorgeous ocean views, a sea cave, a dip in the sea, and the potential for a rewarding hot spring, then this adventure along Ontario Ridge Trail (Sycamore Crest) to Pirate's Cave and Pirate's Cove is for you. If you want to make this a really **EPIC** day, you can tack on riding your bike to/from the hike (see instructions for adventure #4 Avila Beach bike ride) for an extra 15-mile ride. If you add the ride, its best to start/finish at the Sycamore Mineral Springs Resort and do the hike up Sycamore Trail which connects to this loop at the top of Ontario Ridge.

Ontario Ridge Trail (Sycamore Crest) to Pirate's Cave and Pirate's Cove

Steep ascent up Ontario Ridge Trail

This trail is a bit of a butt kicker, especially at the beginning, so plan your timing to avoid the heat. The trail begins with a steep ascent up Sycamore Crest, which

Ontario Ridge Trail (Sycamore Crest) to Pirate's Cave and Pirate's Cove

has several false peaks. Every step improves your views of the sea. Eventually you'll reach the top and the terrain will level out. Look around and take in the views of the Shell Beach coast behind you, Avila Beach in front of you, and See

Canyon's many vineyards to the north. I like to sit in the shade of the big oak tree with the swing to have a snack prior to continuing. Keep walking along the trail as it passes a big cell phone tower and look for the spur that takes you down the north side of the ridge directly to Sycamore Mineral Springs Resort & Spa (this makes for a great side trip and is detailed in adventure #24). Soon you will come to a hill that slopes down toward the parking lot for Pirate's Cave and Pirate's Cove. Work those quads as you walk down the hill and try to not slip and land on your backside.

Once you reach the bottom, walk left along the road to the parking lot and follow the main trailhead in the parking lot that slopes toward the sea. You will soon come to a fork — left leads down to the beach, right travels along the mountain. You will do the left fork on the way back, so for now, stay right. After about a half-mile, you'll come to what is known as Pirate's Cave, which offers a superb view toward Avila.

Heading back along the trail, you now want to take the left fork and drop down to the beach. Welcome to Pirate's Cove, a beautiful stretch of beach. You've been working up a sweat, right? You are dying to cool off, right? You brought your birthday suit, right? All right, then drop trou and go dashing into that cold Pacific Ocean and get refreshed. This is the only nude beach in the area and somehow running into the ocean naked makes you feel more alive and free than just about anything else you can do. If you don't want to take the plunge, that's okay, but at least dip your toes. Nude beach etiquette: Neither stare nor take pictures.

Ontario Ridge Trail (Sycamore Crest) to Pirate's Cave and Pirate's Cove

If you're so modest you don't even want to be amongst bare butts, you can head back to the parking lot and hang a right on the trail that parallels Pirate's Cove from above. This is called Shell Beach Bluff Trail. For those who *can* bear to see naked bodies, walk the entire length of the beach while looking left for the rope ladder area where you can climb up off the beach. At the top of the ridge above the rope ladders, hang a right on the Shell Beach Bluff Trail. Follow this trail until it meets Indio Drive. Hikers should not  trespass on Bluff Drive, which is labeled as a private road and ends at a gate anyway. Follow Indio Drive for a minute and it will turn into El Portal Drive. Follow El Portal Drive back to where you parked your car or bike.

Feeling like your muscles could use some TLC? Head up Shell Beach Road a quarter mile to Avila Hot Springs and go for a relaxing soak. For a more upscale experience, if you didn't incorporate it into your hike already, head away from the freeway and past Avila Hot Springs for a half-mile to Sycamore Mineral Springs Resort & Spa, where you  can rent out your own private hot tub by the hour. Best to make reservations at Sycamore Mineral Springs.

To finish your day, drive to Depalo & Sons to grab a hot sando, some gourmet snacks, something local from their terrific wine selection, and then head down to Dinosaur Caves Park, one of the top spots on the Central Coast to watch the sun set in the Pacific. Find yourself a bench overlooking the sea or plop down on the huge lawn. If it's too chilly outside, the upscale Ventana Grill has amazing views and very good food.

Pismo Preserve

A Jewel of Preserved Land with Spectacular Ocean Views

What to Bring: hat, sunscreen, water, hiking shoes, trekking poles
When to Go: Anytime
Duration/Distance: 3–4 hours

Directions to Start: 101 South to Exit 191B in Pismo Beach. Entrance and parking lot are located on the mountain side of the 101 at the end of Mattie Road.

With more than 900 acres and 10 miles of trails that take you through oaks, over ridgelines, and offer mesmerizing Pacific views, the Pismo Preserve is truly one of the gems of the Central Coast. You can thank the Land Conservancy of San Luis Obispo County for this absolute feat of a preserve. This nonprofit has been working for more than 30 years to protect some of the most beautiful places in SLO so future generations can enjoy them — and this preserve is their crowning achievement to date. The preserve first opened to the public in January 2020. Take my word for it — you want to explore this place and do all 11 miles of trails! So get out there and enjoy!

The parking area is located off Highway 101 on Mattie Road. On the 101 going southbound, exit on Price Road, go right immediately toward Ventana Grill, then turn and go under the freeway to get to Mattie Road, and take the quick right to the Pismo Preserve. If you're going northbound on the 101, exit on Price Road, take your first right on Mattie Road, then right again for the Preserve.

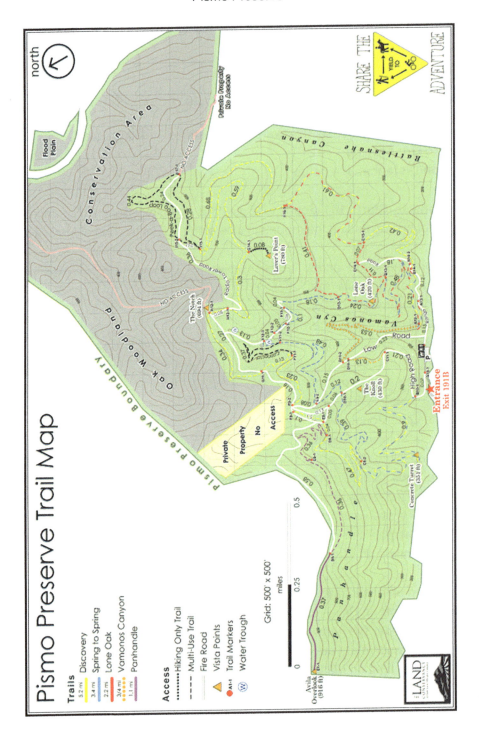

I suggest you plan your day by choosing between making your trip to the Pismo Preserve a morning adventure or afternoon adventure. Mornings are cooler and may have fewer people, but many times the coast is covered in fog. Afternoons are hotter, more crowded, and typically offer clearer views. Depending on the time of day you want to go, you will slightly alter what you do. Let's start with the morning adventure.

Morning Adventure to Pismo Preserve
Start your day with breakfast in downtown Pismo Beach on Price Street around Pismo Avenue. You should be able to satiate your hunger at Penny's All American Cafe, Beachin' Biscuits, or Honeymoon Cafe. If you want something sweeter, head to Old West Cinnamon Rolls, a staple in Pismo Beach.

Pismo Preserve

Head down Main Street, and if you want to check out the Pismo Beach Pier, go for it! Otherwise, go straight to the beach. Walk or run north (right) on the beach for about a mile. Go as far as you can until the cliffs meet the sea and look right for the set of stairs leading up from the beach.

Take these stairs up to a trail that runs behind many clifftop hotels. Continue on the trail all the way to the end, which is the Lighthouse Suites (if you ever want a

Bikers riding in the morning fog

cool place to stay, get one of the ocean-view rooms). Walk through the parking lot to get to Price Street and go left. Walk along Price Street and cross under the freeway across from Ventana Grill. You are now on Mattie Road and can take the first right to enter the Pismo Preserve.

Head into the Preserve and enjoy some EPIC trails. First-timers should do the 5.2-mile Discovery Trail and add other trails as time and energy-levels allow. Mountain biking is allowed and there are special times (see website) when horseback riding is permitted.

Pismo Preserve

As seen in the photos, going to the Preserve when it is foggy has some real drawbacks, namely very little visibility of the ocean that spreads out before you. Assuming you walked along the beach already, perhaps that isn't such a big deal. However, the entire experience is much more worthwhile on a clear day when you can see all of Pismo Beach and the Pismo Pier to the south and Dinosaur Caves and the beach in Avila to the north.

When you come back out, retrace your steps to downtown, perhaps stopping in Ventana Grill for a late lunch or walking all the way back down by the pier so you can go to Splash Café for some clam chowder, Oyster Bar for oysters with a view, or any of the other great restaurants in town.

The Pier in Pismo Beach

Afternoon Adventure to Pismo Preserve

For the afternoon adventure (and a really great date!), check the time of the sunset and make a reservation (preferably a few days in advance) at either Ventana Grill or Oyster Bar for one hour prior to sunset. Start your adventure by having lunch in downtown Pismo Beach. Chop Street and Ada's Fish House are good options, but you can also stroll along Price Street and head down Pomeroy Avenue, and you'll find anything you could possibly want. Do everything discussed above in the morning adventure: check out the pier, walk along the beach, take the steps to the trail behind the hotels, and walk under the freeway to the start of the Pismo Preserve. Enjoy the heck out of the Preserve and plan to be back down with enough time to watch a sunset from your restaurant of choice.

Pismo Preserve

Sunset in Pismo

27

Relax and Reflect in Pismo and Avila

A Day to Relax, Recharge, and Refocus

What to Bring: hat, sunscreen, blanket or towel, this book, pen and paper, water, picnic
When to Go: Anytime
Duration/Distance: A few hours to all day

Directions to Start: Pismo Beach near the pier

Even the most adventurous of us needs a day of relaxation from time to time. And who says relaxation can't be an adventure? Sure, you can Netflix and chill, but that won't charge you up, get you excited about life, and help you reconnect with what matters most to you. Trust me — follow this adventure and you'll be feeling better than you have in a long time.

Start your day with a class at Harmony House Yoga in Pismo Beach. Any class with owner Kelly Metcalf will be particularly wonderful. Walk over to Honeymoon Cafe for a breakfast burrito or a smoothie. Now head down to the beach for a nice long walk or run. You can go about a mile north before the beach runs out, and if you head south, you can go for miles.

Find a spot on the beach that calls to you and take a seat. Get comfortable. Listen to the waves come and go. Think about how your worries come and go. Think about how in one year, five years, and 100 years from now, your worries and anxieties of today will not matter, nor will you remember them. Think about your previous fears and try to consider if they were well founded or if they were just your mind looking for something to do. We humans have an amazing capacity to fantasize and worry about things that usually never happen!

Relax and Reflect in Pismo and Avila

Read this to yourself:

My Rebirth by Jared Friedman

All of my choices have brought me to where I am today
If I want a different tomorrow, I must choose a different way
I have been through much and know more is to come
But I have persevered and have the fortitude to overcome

I forgive those who hurt me
I forgive myself for any I have hurt
I take responsibility for my life

My choices have made me who I am today
Many have made an impression, but I choose which of their lessons will stay
In my heart, my head, my now, my tomorrow,
So much happiness, and yes, also sorrow

I choose my thoughts
I choose to be positive
I choose to be happy
I have so much to feel grateful for

I am reborn every morning
I write my own story
I am able to make lasting change in my life
I commit to myself
I will start right now

Now write down everything you want to improve in your life. This is a good exercise because once you get your worries out of your head, you free up space to think about more positive things. Additionally, once you label these issues and can see them, you can address each one with focus to determine how you can make any desired changes.

Next, spend a few minutes writing everything you're grateful for. This exercise is something you can repeat any day and especially when you are in a crummy mood. Try this activity in relation to someone who has been driving you crazy and see what surprises you find.

All this self-reflection making you hungry? Walk over to Chop Street and grab a bite.

Call ahead to Sycamore Mineral Springs Resort & Spa (see adventure #24 for more details) and make a reservation for a hot tub for yourself for one hour ($20/person per hour). Add a massage if you'd like. Make it early enough that you give yourself enough time to enjoy dinner during sunset. Call ahead to Ventana Grill and make a reservation for 30 minutes prior to sunset or plan to go eat at Mersea's at the pier in Avila where you can watch the sunset while sitting on the water.

Now that you have time until your soak, either walk around Pismo Beach or go take a lovely hike that provides wonderful views of the Pacific. For the hike, check out adventure #25 or #26 if you are staying in Pismo, or select the hike from Sycamore Mineral Springs Resort in chapter #24 if you are going for a soak.

After you've walked, soaked, and watched the sun set while enjoying a great dinner, you should be loose as a goose. But perhaps you are not quite done taking care of #1? If so, head to Happy Feet in SLO on Broad Street (if you haven't already had a massage), and opt for the 30-minute foot massage, which is less than 30 bucks.

Relax and Reflect in Pismo and Avila

Later, as you drift off to sleep, remind yourself that you should do adventures like this more often.

But wait, want to make this day a little more **EPIC**? If it's Tuesday or Wednesday night, head over to the White Heron Sangha in Avila where you can join a guided meditation. A little mindfulness can go a long way. Namaste!

28

Pismo Surfing and Kayaking
Spend a Day on the Water in the Top Tourist Town on the Central Coast

What to Bring: hat, sunscreen, water, picnic
When to Go: Anytime
Duration/Distance: 4+ hours

Directions to Start: 101 South to Pismo Beach, park near the pier

If you attempted the last two adventures, you probably understand by now why many people consider Pismo Beach to be synonymous with the Central Coast. Of all the great towns along the ocean in this part of California, Pismo Beach has the most businesses, most developed coastline, most things to do in town near the water, AND also offers great water activities — especially surfing, boogie boarding, and kayaking. Yes, the water is freezing. Always. But, as with most things outdoors, if you have the right gear, weather conditions don't matter all that much. So grab a thick wetsuit, and let's get in the water!

For this adventure, we're going to focus on surfing and kayaking. If you want to do both in the same day and you go surfing first, you will want to give yourself a break for a few hours after surfing since you will likely be pretty exhausted and need to recharge. While not detailed below, you can swap out surfing or kayaking for scuba diving or stand-up paddle boarding. Both are fun alternatives and you can get everything you need for either at Pismo Beach Dive Shop.

Surfing Pismo Beach
Pismo Beach has consistently good waves that are perfect for beginners, making it one of the best spots along the Central Coast to learn to surf. There are several great surf schools, including Sandbar Surf School, Pismo Beach Surf Academy, Central Coast Surf School, and Zada Surf School. Pick one and call a few days in advance or go online and reserve your spot. They will provide you with all the gear you need, except you'll want to bring a bathing suit, sunscreen, towel, and drinking water. Private lessons are about $100 for two hours. Group lessons are

about $70 for two hours. Since groups are normally pretty small, this might be a good way to save a little money.

For those who have never surfed, you will be amazed at how physically demanding it is. Avid surfers forget to tell newbies how they'll use what feels like thousands of muscles they didn't even know they had. You will be knackered after a few hours of trying to catch waves. Surfing is a combination of freestyle swimming, burpees, and balance. Sounds fun, right? Amazingly, when you put it all together, it is fantastic.

To prepare for your first day of surfing, or to become a better surfer, I will impart you with a simple, but not easy, exercise one of my surfer friends taught me (it's what I wish I had known prior to my first time): Practice lying on the floor, do a pushup, then "pop" your legs under you with one leg in front of the other. Put your arms out for balance … and you are surfing on dry land! Now do this over and over so that it's all one fluid, fast motion. All you'll have left to do is balance on a small board while getting pushed by a wave. Exhilarated? More like exhausted, right? Of course, you can skip this practice and do it all on the water, but the exercise will give you a leg up. (Get it? Even I have to groan at that one.) Do this for a few weeks and you will no doubt be on your way to a chiseled surfer bod. Bodacious!

But, you might ask, what about sharks? Luckily, the Central Coast has seen relatively few incidents with sharks. Still, the risk does exist. According to International Shark Attack File maintained by the Florida Museum, the chance of getting attacked by a shark is 1 in 11.5 million. Meanwhile, the National Weather Service puts the odds of getting struck by lightning at 1 in 1.22 million. If you're really concerned about sharks, according to experts, a few things help: avoid prime feeding time at dusk and dawn, surf in a pack, don't flail, stay away from dead sea life, and stay alert.

Hopefully you caught a few waves while surfing. No doubt you'll be ready to eat after such exertion. A few favorites are Splash Café for their bread bowl clam chowder, Cracked Crab for fish and chips, the Oyster Loft for … you guessed it … oysters, Penny's All American Café for brunch, Papi's Grill for Mexican, Wooly's for burgers and seafood, Central Coast Meat Market for barbeque, and Giuseppe's for pizza and Italian food.

Take a few hours to rest on the beach, drink a lot of water, stretch a bit, take a nap, and recharge. If your arms are too tired, you might want to add elements of adventure #26, Pismo Preserve, to your day. Assuming you can lift your arms, you might just be ready for kayaking.

Kayaking Pismo Beach
The second great water sport in Pismo is kayaking, and a number of shops offer tours. Among them, Central Coast Kayaks and Pismo Beach Dive Shop are both highly rated and great options for folks who've never kayaked before. On a typical kayaking tour, you might spot sea lions, sea otters, dolphins, and even migrating whales (from a distance). This area is really fun and exciting for kayaking since you visit a reef and can travel through sea caves.

If you really want to make your kayak trip **EPIC**, time it during sunset. As you watch the sun dip below the Pacific while on the water, exhausted from a full day of activity, know that you crushed this day and will soon crush a night of deep sleep.

29

Arroyo Grande and Lopez Lake
Off-Grid Morning, Old West Afternoon, and Pacific Sunset Evening

What to Bring: hat, sunscreen, sunglasses, swimsuit, towel, flip-flops, water, picnic, beach chairs, warm layers, wood for bonfire on beach
When to Go: Anytime, but summer is best for water activities
Distance/Duration: 4+ hours

Directions to Start: Start anywhere in downtown SLO

Arroyo Grande (usually abbreviated "AG" and pronounced "a-gee") is one of the "Five Cities" commonly referred to by locals (the others being Pismo Beach, Shell Beach, Grover Beach, and Oceano). With a cute downtown, arguably the best restaurant in the county, access to Grover Beach to the west and Lopez Lake to the northeast, there are easily a few days of activities in the area.

We'll make this adventure a loop by starting with morning activities at Lopez Lake to get a hike in, go to the water park, kayak, fish, or try the ropes course. Then, we'll move on to exploring the historic downtown Village of Arroyo Grande ("The Village"), and we'll end the day with a meal and a sunset over the Pacific.

Lopez Lake
For Lopez Lake (https://slocountyparks.com/camp/lopez-lake/), assuming you're in SLO, go east on Johnson, turn left at Orcutt, then left again as Orcutt meets Tank Farm. Follow the road past some wonderful wineries until it hits a T-intersection and you can choose left for Lopez Lake or right for the Village of Arroyo Grande. Go left on Lopez Road and note Talley Vineyards almost

immediately on your left — this is a great spot to visit after the lake. You'll pass Biddle Regional Park, which is nice but has a day use fee. A few miles of rolling hills later, you'll cross over the dam and enter the Lopez Lake area. Unless you are here to simply hike (see below), you'll want to pay the $10 day use fee to enter at the Lopez Lake Campground entrance.

The canyons of Lopez Lake used to be the hunting and fishing grounds for the Chumash Indians. Today at the lake you get to pick from normal activities — fishing, boating, kayaking, hiking — or man-made activities such as the Mustang Waterpark or the Vista Lago Adventure Park.

Chumash History

According to the Santa Ynez Chumash: https://www.Santaynezchumash.org/history.html, the Chumash once numbered in the tens of thousands and lived along the coast of California from Paso Robles to Malibu and on the Channel Islands. They were hunters, gatherers, and fishermen and lived in large, dome-shaped homes that were made of willow branches. They distinguished themselves as boat builders and learned to seal cracks of their large wooden plank canoes with tar. This allowed them to access the scattered Chumash villages up and down the coastline and on the Channel Islands. As with most Native American tribes, the Chumash history was passed down from generation to generation through stories and legends. Many of these stories were lost when the Chumash Indian population was all but decimated in the 1700s and 1800s by the Spanish mission system mainly due to the introduction of European diseases.

The Mustang Waterpark is great in the summer, especially if you have kids in tow. They'll love the slides and pool. Bring your swimsuit, because you're going to get wet. They also sell food and buckets of beer. While entry is not cheap at about $20 per person, on a hot day, it's totally worth the price. Remember to bring your own towel. You are allowed to bring in water, too. (As if they didn't have plenty.) They give you a wristband so you can enter and exit as you like, so don't forget that picnic if you want to exit the park and eat rather than buy the food on site!

The Vista Lago Adventure Park has a really good ropes course and fun zip

Arroyo Grande and Lopez Lake

lines. Conveniently, if you happen to be camping at the lake, you can just walk over.

Speaking of camping, there are more than 350 sites available at the campground, with many overlooking the water and some in the oaks.

High Ridge Trail

There is a $10 fee to enter the Lopez Lake Campground , so if all you want to do is hike, you can avoid the fee by going right on Hi Mountain Road just before the park entrance, turning left on Upper Lopez Canyon Road, then driving to the top of the ridge and parking at any of the shoulder pull-offs. This positions you right on one of the main hikes — the High Ridge Trail Loop. You'll get a great feeling for the area and there are lots of different variations depending on how far  you want to go. If you do this hike during the week, chances are you'll have the place all to yourself. Go in a counterclockwise direction and when you get to the campground by the lake, if there are too many people for your liking, head up one of the spurs to the upper trail where you started so you get the *killer views* in the opposite direction. Like many hikes on the Central Coast, you'll want to watch out for poison oak and ticks.

If you're pressed for time, do the first small loop, which is about a mile. Use the Bobcat and Turkey Ridge trails since they connect to the High Ridge Trail. The full 4.7-mile hike is shown in the map on the preceeding page, but as you can see, there are many options to shorten the hike.

Village of Arroyo Grande
Next up, head to the Village of AG. You will be forgiven if you stop at Talley Vineyards along the way — it's one of the best in the area. Perhaps pick up a bottle for later in the day? In the summer you get the bonus of being able to stop off at their farm stand for their wonderful produce.

In AG, park on Branch Street anywhere around Bridge Street or Mason Street. Stop in at some of the antique shops and score a unique find. There are plenty of good eats too, including the Mason Bar and Kitchen, Planted, Rooster Creek Tavern, and Klondike Pizza. The original Doc Burnstein's is beloved by Slocals, too. Make a quick jaunt down Short Street. If it's a Saturday morning, look for the farmers' market. Otherwise, go over the hanging bridge through Centennial Park. Continue on the small path over the Arroyo Grande River to Heritage Square Park. On Sundays in the summer, you may encounter an old-timey band playing and folks getting down. Get in there and show them what you got. Dance like nobody knows you.

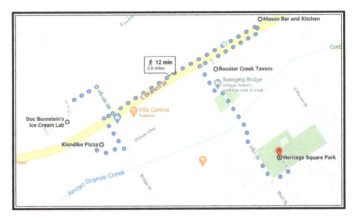

To continue the loop, head west on Grand Avenue to cruise through the main drag of AG. You will quickly pass over Highway 101, and shortly thereafter, you will pass Ember Restaurant on the right, one of the best restaurants in SLO County. If you're not there early, expect to wait probably longer than you want. A few doors down is Figueroa Mountain Brewing, the best brewery in AG. If you didn't grab wine earlier at Talley, consider grabbing a few 22s for the beach. You will soon cross over Oak Park Boulevard, which takes you out of AG and into Grover Beach. If you haven't sorted out dinner yet, now's the time. You can stop in at one of the many great restaurants along Grand Avenue, or else take your food to go and head to the beach. As you pass 3rd Street, The Spoon Trade is on the right, and, for my money, is right up there with Ember for the title of Best Food on Grand Avenue — and perhaps in the county!

Peanuts on the floor at Klondike Pizza

Grover Beach

As you pass over Highway 1, there is a big parking lot on the right, or you can drive your car down onto the beach. I am very hesitant to encourage you to drive on the beach although I will say that this is the last place in the state where you can and it will be made illegal in the coming years so if your life won't be complete otherwise, now is your chance. When the beach is packed with cars, you're better off with four-wheel drive if you want to minimize your chance of getting stuck. As a cheapskate, I avoid the fee for driving onto the beach by instead parking in the lot and then walking down to the beach with my dinner and drinks. But if your vehicle and wallet allows, pay the fee and drive on one of the last beaches in California where it's permitted. Now you have everything you need with you, so take a nice walk, drop a few logs into the sand, start a warm fire, and enjoy a beautiful sunset before heading home.

The Santa Ynez Valley Loop

"Best Of" Counterclockwise Loop of Los Alamos, Buellton, Solvang, Santa Ynez, Ballard, and Los Olivos

What to Bring: hat, sunscreen, water, picnic set
When to Go: All year is great, summers can be hot
Duration/Distance: Day Trip

Directions to Start: Drive from SLO south on the 101 to Los Alamos

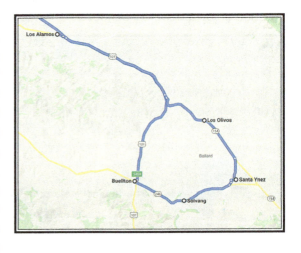

What does a Dutch village, Ostrich farm, miniature horses, and lots of wine have in common? You can find all of them on The Santa Ynez Valley loop. This lovely region about 30 minutes north of Santa Barbara gets more tourists than you normally see in SLO County. Even so, with its broad, open fields, clear skies, and relatively easy travel, you'll still feel worlds away from the "big city" of Santa Barbara. Prior to heading down, you should do two things: 1) Watch the movie *Sideways* which features this area, and 2) Go to the visit Santa Ynez website https://www.visitsyv.com/events/?syv_filter=special to see if anything special is going on during your planned visit. This adventure is less likely to get your blood flowing and more likely to get the liquids flowing, so consider it an urban adventure.

The Santa Ynez Valley is made up of five communities: Solvang, Los Olivos, Santa Ynez, Buellton, and Ballard. For this adventure, I threw in their cool northern neighbor, Los Alamos as a bonus.

The Santa Ynez Valley Loop

There's a lot packed in to this loop, so don't feel bad if you never make it past the first few stops on the tour. That'll just give you reason to come back! You could easily break this adventure into three to five days, which I've done in the next three chapters, so check those out for more in-depth information about each town if you'd like to linger a bit.

Los Alamos

Starting from SLO, drive south on the 101 to Los Alamos and get off on Bell Street. At the stop sign, go left. Make mental notes of anything you might want to come back and see in a subsequent adventure or for dinner as you drive through the center of this small but lovely town. Head to Bob's Well Bread Bakery and grab yourself anything that looks good since everything tastes as good as it looks. Grab a coffee to go and perhaps walk across the street to the Depot Mall, a massive antique shop, then meander up and down the main drag.

Hop in your car and head south to the 101 South. After about 15 minutes exit in Buellton.

Buellton

If you're hungry, go directly to Industrial Eats for an early lunch before they get too packed. Try something different like the smoked pheasant salad. If you're not hungry, there's a lot of fun spots for wine or beer: The Loring Wine Company

(which has a nice wine and cookie pairing), Buscador Winery and Tasting Room, Helix: The Evolution of Wine, Standing Sun Winery, Figueroa Brewing, and

Firestone Barrel Works. If you don't feel like boozing, check out the Santa Ynez Valley Botanic Garden in the beautiful River View Park.

Now, take Highway 246 east. In about 10 minutes you'll see Ostrichland on your right. If you've never seen an ostrich up close, it's probably worth a stop. Otherwise, give those birds the bird and continue on to Solvang.

Solvang
Solvang is a must-do daytrip if you're on the Central Coast for any amount of time. For those who haven't traveled much outside the U.S., the town will feel unique, quaint, and pretty. For those who have, it will likely feel contrived and touristy. Either way, there are some spots worth checking out that are sure to please even the most experienced and cynical traveler.

The Santa Ynez Valley Loop

As you enter Solvang, park anywhere after you see your first Dutch bakery. Walk along Mission Drive, then meander through the few streets to the south — mainly Park Way and Copenhagen Drive. A few good spots to check out include Hanson's Clock Shop Jewelers, the free Hans Christian Andersen Museum, and a solid coffee shop called the Good Seed Coffee Co. While I haven't found anything too compelling at either Paula's Pancake House or Olsen's Danish Village Bakery, just about everyone who comes through town stops at one or the other. The spot you want for an aebleskiver is Solvang Restaurant (which you'll know by the line). What's an aebleskiver, you might ask? I'd tell you, but then I'd have to kill you. Try one and find out. For one of the best meals in town, go where the locals go: Haven Hill Provisions, which is great for either lunch or dinner. Maybe grab a T-shirt at G. Wilikers. Old Mission Santa Ines is particularly well preserved and worth a stop if you like missions.

Hop back in the car and head east on Mission Drive and Highway 246 toward Santa Ynez.

Santa Ynez
This town has an Old West vibe and a few legit places to eat, including The Lucky Hen Larder, the deli at the Santa Ynez Valley Cheese Company, or S.Y. Kitchen, which has one of the best dinners around. Brothers Restaurant at the Red Barn is really popular. If you are a bread freak, you'll love The Baker's Table. Consider picking up something to bring home to make toast or French toast.

Ballard
As you continue your loop, perhaps make a brief stop to see the unbelievably cute miniature horses at Quicksilver Ranch at 1555 Alamo Pintado Road. And since you're right there, it's worth stopping just next door at Lincourt Vineyards.

Heading north, if it's June or July or you just love lavender, go to the Clairmont Lavender Farm. Otherwise, keep on going until you get to the lovely, walkable little town of Los Olivos.

Los Olivos

This tightly packed town has a lot worth seeing and doing, especially if you like gourmet food or wine. With so many options, you should just stroll and pick the one that calls to you. Some great options are: Saarloos & Sons, Community Craft, Kaena Tasting Room, Refugio Ranch, Carhartt Vineyards, and Dreamcote Wines. If you want something nonalcoholic, go to Olive Hill Farm to taste both olive oil and balsamic vinegar. And if you're looking for a good spot for dinner, you can finish off your **EPIC** day with either The Bear and Star or the Los Olivos Wine Merchant & Cafe.

Los Alamos and Buellton

The Drive to LA Just Got Way Better

What to Bring: hat, sunscreen, water, frisbee
When to Go: Thursday through Sunday all year is great, summers can be hot
Duration/Distance: Day Trip

Directions to Start: South from SLO on 101, get off at Bell Street in Los Alamos

In this adventure, we're going to explore two up-and-coming towns that seem to change (for the better) every visit. Either town makes for a great day trip, and if you need to head south to LA or Santa Barbara, you also can't go wrong making a detour to one of them.

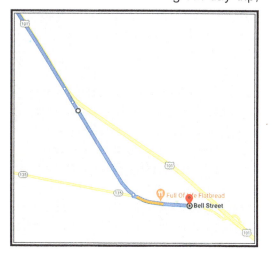

Starting from SLO, drive to Los Alamos and get off at the first exit for Bell Street. Go left at the stop sign, and you will be on the main drag through town. Keep in mind that, with the exception of maybe a few stores, most of Los Alamos is closed Monday through Wednesday.

Los Alamos

Los Alamos looks like a hipster Old West town that could have been designed by *Sunset* magazine. You will want to check out almost every spot here. With its art shops, gift stores, and restaurants, there are more places in this half-mile stretch of town than most places 10 times the size. You could easily spend the entire day here, and if you decide to throw the rest of this adventure out the window and stick around for a while, I won't hold it against you.

There is wonderful wood-fired pizza at Full of Life Flatbread; beer and wine to be enjoyed on recliners next to a firepit or while playing bocce ball at The Bodega; lovely Victorian B&Bs, a cool old saloon at the Union Hotel called the 1880 Union Saloon; to-go tacos and other treats from Vallefresh; French dining at Bell's; an outdoor beer garden at Babis; very inviting wine tasting rooms at Casa Dumetz Wines, Municipal Winemakers and Bedford Winery; a good little sit-down breakfast and coffee at Plenty; and finally, a monstrous antique shop called Depot Mall across from a killer bakery called Bob's Well Bread Bakery.

Full of Life Flatbread

Let's spend a moment on Bob's Well Bread Bakery since this place is a standout and has mouthwatering menu items, such as their perfectly made croissant, chocolate croissant, almond croissant, and almond croissant with chocolate — and that's just the croissants! There is so much more, including many types of coffee drinks. You'll want to try every one of the nearly dozen styles of their fresh baked breads! The line is regularly out the door and waits can be 30 minutes or more, but it's worth it!

Thrown in a few art shops and gifts stores and simply put, there are more go-to spots in this half-mile stretch of town than most places 10 times the size. You could easily spend the whole day here and if you want to earn extra genius points, perhaps throw the rest of this adventure out the window, grab a room at a B&B and stick around for a while.

Find a hidden treasure at the Depot Mall

If you're in a hurry and want to take a quick look-see around the town, simply do what I do when I'm driving from SLO to LA and make the easy exit on Bell Street, stop at Bob's Well Bread Bakery, then keep on keeping on. If you're driving from LA to SLO, drop in at Full of Life Flatbread. If you have a little more time on your hands perhaps go south in the middle of town on Centennial Street and head to Los Alamos County Park which is a good place to stretch your legs and/or have a picnic.

Buellton

Fifteen minutes south of Los Alamos on the 101 and you'll hit Buellton, which has historically been more of a pass-through town for folks heading to the Santa Ynez Valley or just stopping for gas. Nowadays, it has a lot to offer, with seemingly better options all the time.

In the event you skipped Los Alamos or didn't yet eat, head straight to Pattibakes for some delicious baked goods or a breakfast sandwich, or go to Ellen's Danish Pancake House, where you have to try the, you guessed it, Danish pancakes. Or, especially with kids in tow, you may want to head to family-friendly Mother Hubbards, which offers yummy, locally sourced breakfast and lunch, including a good corned beef hash! Of course, there's also

the historic Pea Soup Andersen's. It's definitely touristy, but many people love this place and highly recommend the Cobb salad and the pea soup. I don't really like Cobb salads and I despise peas, so I'll have to take their word for it. If you want to know more about the town, the Buellton Historical Society is located above Pea Soup Andersen's.

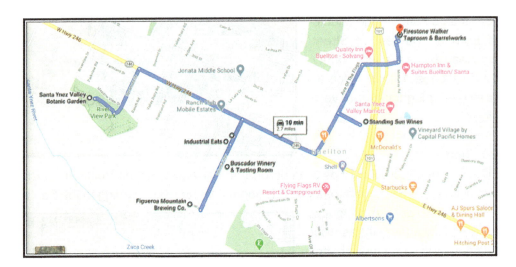

For my money, if I'm in Buellton, I'd prefer a meal at Industrial Eats any day of the week. I also mentioned this stop in the previous adventure if you are doing the Santa Ynez Valley loop. Located in what looks like industrial buildings, the aptly named Industrial Eats is cool, delicious, and loved by locals for offering both the traditional foods you know and love (like pizza) and creations you never knew you loved (like smoked pheasant salad). Industrial Eats gets packed, so try to plan for an early or late lunch. Or, better yet, if you do have to wait, do yourself a favor and grab some wine first across the parking lot at the Loring Wine Company. I especially enjoy their wine and cookie pairing. Next door to Loring Wine, there was a great little gift shop worth checking out, although I've seen that places in this industrial area seem to move out as quickly as they pop up. So take a walk around and see what's new and perhaps walk around the corner to get some spirits at Dorwood Distillery.

If you're a beer lover, you'll want to hit both Figueroa Brewing and Firestone Barrel Works in Buellton prior to leaving town. Both have food and Fig has bocce ball and oversized Jenga. If wine is more your thing, you'll want to make stops at Buscador Winery and Tasting Room, its neighbor Helix: The Evolution of Wine, and east a few blocks to Standing Sun Winery. Want to stick with spirits? Go just south to Ascendant Spirits.

One really lovely spot you may want to check out that was built by the community for the community is the Santa Ynez Valley Botanic Garden in the beautiful River View Park. Head over to see local plants in a relaxing setting. The park itself has a lot to offer also, and if you have kids, they will love all the fun activities like the maze, trails and playground. If you brought a frisbee, now is the chance to work on your Hammer throw.

Before leaving Buellton, in the event you have a little one to shop for, get a unique present at ONEderchild Children's Gifts & Consignment at 240 E Hwy 246.

If you want to extend your time in the area, a fun option for an overnight stay is at a relatively new place called Flying Flags. This upscale campground has camping, a RV site, glamping cabins, Airstreams, and safari tents. The grounds are lovely and there is plenty to do for the kids.

To round out the trip, you may want to head back to Los Alamos for dinner on your way back north. Full of Life Flatbread has some of the best pizza on the Central Coast. Or continue heading toward SLO and consider stopping off for a bite or drink with a view of the ocean in Pismo. There's the perpetually busy Splash Café right by the water where you can get some deliciously buttery clam chowder, or you can go upscale and head to Ventana Grill, which is one of the top eateries in the county to enjoy a sunset.

Los Olivos and Santa Ynez

Lovely Small Towns with Big things to Offer, Especially for Food and Wine Aficionados

What to Bring: hat, sunscreen, water, sunglasses, hiking shoes, trekking poles, picnic
When to Go: All year is great, summers can be hot
Duration/Distance: Day Trip

Directions to Start: 101 South to 154 East to Los Olivos
From SLO, head directly to Los Olivos for breakfast. Then, head to Santa Ynez and loop back through Ballard to Los Olivos.

Los Olivos

Founded in 1887 after the Pacific Coast Railway began operating, Los Olivos is a happening little town and is highly walkable. It's sleepy in the morning but really livens up at night, in part because of all its tasting rooms and wine and beer joints. See for yourself and experience both sides of this great place. This is the town you'll want to come back to time and again. In fact, you'll *have* to come back, because there is so much listed in this adventure, there's just no way to do it 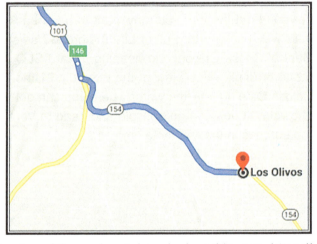 all in one day. To see the wineries of the region, take a look at this map: https://www.visitsyv.com/wp-content/uploads/2014/03/SYVDG-2017-Winery-Map-PDF-copy.pdf.

The center of town is at the cross streets of Grand Avenue and Alamo Pintado Avenue. If you arrive in time for breakfast or brunch, try the farm-to-table restaurant The Bear and Star (7am–9pm) located on the corner of Grand Avenue and Hollister Street. Their menu changes with the seasons, so there's always something new and delicious to try. This is also one of your best options for coffee in town.

If you want to get a workout in, you have two good options detailed below which both start from the same place: 1) The moderate 3.8-mile Lover's Loop via Grass Mountain Trail or, 2) The hard 4.5-mile Grass Mountain Trail. Since you have to travel through town to get to the road leading to the hikes, you can eat then hike, or hike then eat. How's that for convenience?

Lover's Loop via Grass Mountain Trail

For those of you who really want to get a hike in, grab breakfast first thing and then head out to Lover's Loop via Grass Mountain Trail. This 3.8-miler is about a 12-minute drive north of Los Olivos. You'll want to do the hike counterclockwise so you end it on the downslope. Take plenty of water, especially in the summer. During the wildflower blooms in April or May, this hike gets even more spectacular.

To get to the trailhead, use this address as your destination: 5100 Figueroa Mountain Rd, Santa Ynez, CA 93460. Take Figueroa Mountain Road north from Los Olivos. Look left during the last mile of the drive, as you are minutes from Michael Jackson's Neverland Ranch. In case you're wondering, it's closed to the public, but you can go as far as the front gate and then moonwalk your way back to your car and get hiking!

Grass Mountain Trail

If you want a butt-kicker of a hike, pull out your trekking poles and get ready for a real knee wobbler. You'll start in the same place as the previous hike and go clockwise for about 0.7 miles before the trail forks left from Lover's Loop. Grass Mountain Trail is "only" 4.5 miles, but it is 2,411 feet of elevation gain in 2.25 miles to the peak of Grass Mountain, then all the way back down. Don't take this hike on lightly — you need plenty of water, sun protection, good hiking shoes, *and* you'll be thankful you have trekking poles if you're smart enough to bring them. Doing this hike during the wildflower bloom in April/May (check local reports) is especially amazing.

To get to the trailhead, follow the same directions as for Lover's Loop above. In fact, you follow the first 0.7 miles of Lover's Loop in the clockwise direction, continue more or less straight when Lover's Loop goes right, and make your way to the top. You have the option of doing Lover's Loop after coming back down from the peak of Grass Mountain. This will bring your total hike closer to 7 miles.

Now head back to Los Olivos.

Los Olivos

After filling your belly and/or heading out for a hike, explore the town going up and down Grand Avenue,

the main drag. You may want to head to Pedego Electric Bikes for an easy and fun way of checking out the town. Otherwise, you'll get a few miles in as you walk through town, which will make you feel much less guilty about all the calories you're going to consume during your visit.

Additionally, the Santa Ynez Valley Historical Society designed a walking tour that focuses on the buildings throughout town. (You can reference it here: https://www.losolivosca.com/wp-content/uploads/2016/04/LOWalkingTour_web.pdf.) Perhaps pair that with the walking tour I suggest below, which focuses on shops, food, and other commercial highlights.

Los Olivos Walking Tour

Let's start our walking tour of town after parking near The Bear and Star. Walk east on Hollister to San Marcos Avenue and go left (north). As you head up the street, if you want to grab a great beer or wine at a hidden gem, head to Community Craft at 2446 Alamo Pintado Ave, Suite C.

On the other side (east side) of Alamo Pintado, at the corner, you can get your chocolate fix at Stafford's Chocolates.

Continuing up San Marcos, you might want to drop in at Dreamcote Wines on the left prior to Jonata Street then go left on Jonata Street (or right to Pedego Electric Bikes).

From your left at Jonata, take the first right, where you can dip in to either Epiphany Cellars or Refugio Ranch Vineyards Tasting Rooms. Wrap left on the dirt road for Grand Avenue.

Heading south on Grand Avenue, you'll pass the extremely friendly and well run Saarloos & Sons, which has a great wine and cupcake pairing and plenty of outdoor seating. If you are only going to visit one winery in town, this should be it!

Continuing south on Grand Avenue, cross over Jonata Street as you make your way to the center of town. You have another great tasting option at Carhartt Vineyards ... or keep on keeping on. Just before Alamo Pintado Avenue, mix it up a little at Olive Hill Farm, where you can taste a dozen flavors of both olive oil and balsamic vinegar.

At Grand Avenue and Alamo Pintado Avenue, you are at the center of town. Go west, young reader, if you are ready for lunch at the oddly named Sides Hardware and Shoes (11:30am–3pm). I know

the name makes you think of a leather tanning shop, but it actually was a hardware store back in the day. Today, with offerings like calamari, pork belly tacos, carrot curry soup, pastrami on rye (unbelievably delish), and fried chicken sandos with bacon, your taste buds are in for a real experience. What I'm saying is you can't *screw* up your order because they really *nail* the offerings here. Excuse me, can I get a side of WD-40 to stop the groaning from those puns? **SLOcals Only pro tip:** If you have young kids or if Sides has a wait, you may want to ask if they'll make your order to go and then take it across the street to picnic like a pro at the tiny Lavinia Campbell Park.

While waiting for your food to be prepared, walk a few doors west to the great little nursery J Woeste (10am–5pm), where you will be hard-pressed to leave without a new plant.

Head back to Grand Avenue and perhaps cross over to Kaena Tasting Room on the east side of the road. Continue south and you'll get back to where you started at the Bear and Star.

Onward to Santa Ynez!

Santa Ynez
Given that you may have heard the entire region referred to as the Santa Ynez Valley, you will not be the first to arrive in the town of Santa Ynez and think, "This is it?" While small, this welcoming town has a few places you don't want to miss if you're hungry. The Lucky Hen Larder is a great little deli at the Santa Ynez Valley Cheese Company, which has indoor and outdoor seating. S.Y. Kitchen has one of the best dinners around offering delicious Italian food. Brothers Restaurant at the Red Barn is really popular. For a good breakfast and lunch spot, or if you're a bread freak, you'll love The Bakers Table, which also has good coffee. Another solid coffee option is Pony Espresso. Assuming you want something other than food and you like stagecoaches, you'll want to go to the Santa Ynez Valley Historical Museum and Parks-Janeway Carriage House.

Los Olivos and Santa Ynez

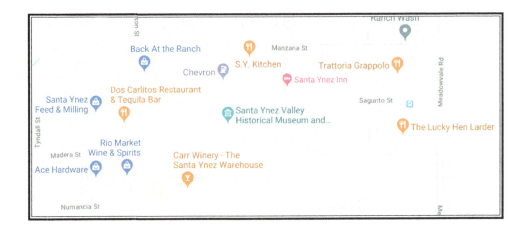

The closest thing to a center of town is Sagunto Street between Edison Street and Faraday. Everything else you might want to see is within a block or two in any direction.

There are more than a dozen wineries within 10 minutes of Santa Ynez. If you have time for only one, consider the popular Sunstone Vineyards, which is reminiscent of Tuscany and offers tasty wines, a great atmosphere, and a family zone with bocce and cornhole.

Now that you've seen Santa Ynez, let's begin making our way back to where we started the day. Head north on Edison Street toward the 154 and check out Arroyo Arabians, then drive up the street to Summerset Farm & Dales Nursery where they have lovely picturesque grounds, great jams, and you can pick your own berries.

Next up … mini donkeys, chickens, geese, piggies, oh my! But wait, what's that? A zonkey?? Yes, they even have a zebra/donkey mix! If it's Saturday between 11 a.m. and 3 p.m. and you have kids with you, you have to stop at Seein' Spots Farm at 2599 Baseline Ave., Solvang, where you can hold, pet, and enjoy animals to your heart's content. Hopefully Turbo, the giant tortoise and part-time escape artist, is still there to dispel all misconceptions about tortoises being slow.

More animals await — and this time they are bigger yet little. I'm talking about miniature horses of courses. If you're in to that sort of thing, make a brief detour to Quicksilver Ranch where you can pay a free visit to miniature horses at 1555 Alamo Pintado Rd, Solvang, CA 93463. Just next door is Lincourt Vineyards, which has good wines and a nice tasting area. It's worth a stop since you're right there.

If you want to bring home a gift, a good stop is the serene Clairmont Lavender Farm. Look for the lavender field on your right as you drive in, but remember, like any other thing that blooms, you have to time it right. Don't blame the lavender for not being in bloom if you show up in January. The actual bloom is dependent on weather, but June or July is normally the best time to go.

If you are ready for more wine, and it is between noon and 5 p.m., continue east to Vincent Vineyards at 2370 N Refugio Rd, Santa Ynez, CA 93460. Otherwise, head back to Grand Avenue and go north to the center of Los Olivos. Now's your chance to see Los Olivos' night life. Check out anywhere you might have skipped earlier in the day. For a great dinner option, go to the Los Olivos Wine Merchant & Café.

The Foxen Canyon Wine Trail

But wait, there's more! Yes, this day is already too **EPIC** and there's no more space, but an alternative option for your day in the region is to grab breakfast in Los Olivos, perhaps do a hike, then follow The Foxen Canyon Wine Trail toward Santa Maria. This gorgeous drive is a terrific alternative to taking the 101 North and makes for a beautiful detour on a trip back to SLO from Santa Barbara or Los Angeles.

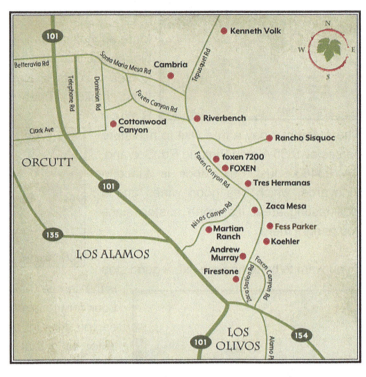

There are 14 wineries along the way, run by some of the best winemakers in the area. This is prime picnicking, so make sure you bring some goodies with you.

Finally, since after doing this adventure once, you'll want to do countless other iterations, keep an eye on the Sedgwick Reserve. This world-class conservation and research facility is normally closed to the public but offers docent-led hikes several times per year. Snag a spot fast if you see one, and then enjoy your time in the 9-square-mile reserve teeming with animal and plant life:
https://www.visitsyv.com/wp-content/uploads/2014/03/SYVDG-2017-Winery-Map-PDF-copy.pdf

Solvang

A little piece of Denmark in Central California

What to Bring: hat, sunscreen, water, good walking shoes
When to Go: All year (summers can be hot)
Duration/Distance: Day Trip

Directions to Start: 101 South to Buellton, east on Highway 246 to Solvang

Solvang (which means "sunny field") is a very touristy Danish town that has been offering Danishes to hordes of tourists for more than a hundred years. If you're in the region for any amount of time, you have to go. It's a certified crowd-pleaser.

But even though this town is what draws most people to the Santa Ynez Valley in the first place, this will probably be the last place in the Valley you'll want to return. Not because Solvang isn't fun, but Solvang has become a bit of a victim of its own success. In the beginning, it more closely resembled the home its original inhabitants came from but, over time, it has drawn so many people its mainstay these days is catering to tourists. Nowadays, Solvang feels more like Disneyland with all its souvenir shops and subpar food. But, also like Disneyland, Solvang has a magic to it and plenty of redeeming qualities (and good food) if you know where to look.

As you approach Solvang from Highway 101, you'll see Ostrichland, which may be a good way to start your day. It's a bit odd, mostly because ostriches are some strange birds. If you're like me, you'll share that common bond with them and enjoy your time together. If that's not your cup of tea, drive on by.

Solvang

A few minutes before Ostrichland and Solvang, you will pass the famed Hitching Post II. Its popularity soared since being featured in the movie *Sideways*, so if you want to eat there, you should make a reservation well in advance. Additionally, the restaurant has an area specific to great wine tasting with especially good pinot noirs!

Visiting Solvang is pretty straightforward; the primary area you'll want to see is walkable and only covers two main streets (Copenhagen and Park) and several cross streets. The town is best visited early so you can get a parking spot prior to boatloads of tourists showing up. While restaurants abound and every bakery looks amazing, the quality of most is subpar at best. My tour outlines many of the spots that make the grade for quality.

Solvang Walking Tour
Most of the highlights of Solvang can be seen easily by foot. The main street through town is Mission Drive and the majority of sights you'll want to visit are south of Mission Drive on Copenhagen Drive and Park Way which both run parallel to Mission Drive. For this walking tour, it's best to park at the Mission Santa Ines.

Ostrichland!

Solvang

Mission Santa Ines

If you like to visit missions at all, you will enjoy this one. Entrance is $5 each or free for kids younger than 12. This well-preserved mission has a small museum with displays on the history of the mission and the Chumash people which really helps you envision life for the first peoples and how people used to be so in tune with the land. There's a nice garden and a public restroom. This is still an operating church so Sundays can be crowded and you will need to wait between mass to see the Mission Church. There are events throughout the year. Find more information here: https://missionsantaines.org/mission]

Downtown Solvang

When you're ready, head west to Alisol Road where you hit the main downtown area, and hang a right at the windmill on the corner. Pop into Hanson's Clock Shop. Continue on to Mission Drive and go west (left). A few doors down, you will reach the very small and free Hans Christian Andersen Museum. There's a good used bookstore called Book Loft attached and a quaint little coffee shop as well. If you like fairytales and/or books, you'll like this museum, which won't take more than twenty minutes tops to visit.

If you want the best coffee around, continue west on Mission Drive for Good Seed Coffee Co., which is sure to please even the most discerning coffee snob.

You can also find many gluten-free and vegan pastry options there. I like the breakfast bowl, which includes free-range eggs, organic cheese, and handmade hash browns. The cinnamon rolls are also quite good.

One of many bakeries in town where everything looks delicious

Considered a staple in town, Paula's Pancake House is recommended in just about every guidebook for Solvang. However, I would give it an average rating and would only go if you really love pancakes and there's no wait.

Like Paula's Pancake House, many people rave about Olsen's Danish Village Bakery and will not leave town without stopping in and grabbing a pastry, loaf of pumpernickel, or insert your favorite item here. I've stopped in several times and never found anything that stands out — not even their pumpernickel bread — so the search for a go-to item continues.

Solvang

On a nice day, a really good option is the outdoor eatery Copenhagen Sausage Garden, which has good sausages and really good soft pretzels with cheese on the side.

Now that you're fed, consider checking out The Elverhøj Museum of History & Art (to learn about the town's history), or visit the Solvang Vintage Motorcycle Museum.

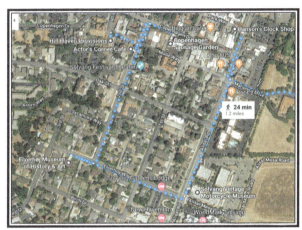

Walk around and check out shops, grab an Æbleskiver, which is a Danish pastry. The spot for Æbleskivers seems to be right next to the Solvang Restaurant where there usually is a line. Check out some of the shops, including a good T-shirt shop called G. Wilikers.

Now that you've done the best of Solvang, want to walk off some of that Danish without being surrounded by hordes of tourists? If so, head for a quick hike at the nearby Hans Christian Andersen Park or Sunny Fields Park.

Hans Christian Andersen Park
For a pleasant 1.7-mile stroll, with only 104 feet of elevation gain, head over to Hans Christian Andersen Park, located just north of Mission Drive, slightly west of downtown. From Olsen's Danish Village Bakery, go about a block west and you'll see the park. This easy walk is a great option for families.

If you have kids, you might opt for Sunny Fields Park instead which caters a bit more to little ones.

Sunny Fields Park

Sunny Fields Park is located just east of town and is a good stop if you have kids with you who need to run around freely. To get there, drive less than a mile east of downtown on 246 and go left on Alamo Pintado Road.

Sunstone Vineyards and Winery

Located five miles southeast of downtown, this lovely winery offers a gorgeous setting to enjoy some wonderful wine and is a highly recommended side trip.

Dinner and a Show?

Ending your day in Solvang with dinner and a show is a special way to make the day even more memorable. Check the schedule for http://www.solvangfestivaltheater.org/ and plan your entire day around a show. If you snag a ticket, have a romantic meal prior to the show at Actor's Corner Cafe (Th–Sun 5–8pm) across from the theater.

If you skip the show, go where the locals go: Haven Hill Provisions, which is great for either lunch or dinner. Or, if you made reservations, eat a meal fit for royalty back at Hitching Post II.

As you head home, smile as you feel like you just traveled to a very busy town in Europe with most of the culture but avoiding all of the jet lag.

34

Lompoc and Vandenberg

Great Wineries, a Mission That Transports You Back in Time, Hiking, Beaches, and Flowers Galore!

What to Bring: hat, sunscreen, water, picnic, warm layers including a windbreaker
When to Go: Apr–Sept for flower fields, rest of year for beaches
Duration/Distance: Day trip with several hiking options

Directions to Start: From SLO, take 101 South to Los Alamos

Adventure Agenda	Option 1	Option 2
Breakfast	Eat at home	Bob's Well Bread
Morning Adventure	Santa Rita mountain bike ride and wine Tasting	La Purisima Mission and State Historic Park
Lunch	Sissy's Uptown Café, Central Coast Specialty Foods, Angela's	Picnic at the Mission
Afternoon	Bike past flower fields or visit Burton Mesa Ecological Reserve	Wine Ghetto, Horse sanctuary or Aquatic Center
Sunset	From PCH while driving	Surf Beach, Ocean Beach Park
Dinner	Jocko's, The (original) Hitching Post	Ada's Fish House

Lompoc and Vandenberg

This adventure is a sprawling exploration of the Lompoc area, and is packed with more things than can realistically be done in a day. Lompoc is about an hour south of SLO on the western side of the 101. The agenda at the top of this chapter shows just two of the many potential ways you can put together an **EPIC** day in the area. Pick the options that sound best to you and keep in mind some will require you to reserve in advance and some are only available during certain times of the year. And for space nuts, you will definitely want to plan some time for space-related activities around Vandenberg.

From SLO, take 101 South and get off at Los Alamos, perhaps stop in at Bob's Well Bread for a chocolate almond croissant, then take the paved-but-rough Drum Canyon Road over the Santa Rita Mountains. This is certainly one of the most off-the-beaten-path routes you can take to Lompoc. I like it because it makes this adventure a loop and takes you off the beaten path, which feels much more adventurous.

Santa Rita Mountains from Los Alamos Toward Lompoc
Consider bringing any ole bike along and riding down from the top of the hill/mountain as you pass over the Santa Rita Mountains to any of the first several wineries listed below. While the driver of the vehicle will not get to bike down the hill, they will have the enviable task of heading to the winery first and checking out the quality. Teenagers may especially appreciate letting parents go ahead as they ride down.

As you come down Drum Canyon Road, the first winery you'll pass that may be worth a stop is Dierberg Vineyard at 1280 Drum Canyon Road. Continue on to Highway 246 and go west (right) toward the ocean. You will soon pass three solid wineries on the right: Foley Estates, Melville Vineyards, and Babcock Winery. Foley offers a cheese and wine pairing with the food coming from local artisans and bakeries. Melville and Babcock are next door to each other and are very highly regarded.

La Purisima Mission and State Historic Park
Now it's time to get your history and hiking fix at La Purisima Mission and State Historic Park. In addition to over 25 miles of hiking trails, this is arguably the best restoration of a mission in California and gives a very real glimpse into daily life of the early settlers in the region. Unlike many other missions you may see that have become the center of town, this rustic mission was built up from the land around it by the Chumash Indians and the Spanish, and the surroundings are as they were 200 years ago when construction took place. If you like missions even a little, you will like this. If you don't care about missions at all but like hiking

or history or native gardening or how to build out of clay or how olive oil used to be made, you will like this. If none of that speaks to you, you, my friend, are hard to please. Hours are 9am–5pm and the worthwhile visitor center is open 10am–4pm. Parking is $6 per vehicle or $5 if you have someone 62 or over with you. If the entrance kiosk is empty, look for the pay machine and put the receipt on your dash. **SLOcals Only Pro Tip:** Some people park just across Purisima Road on Mission Gate Road to avoid the parking fee.

La Purisima Mission

In addition to the historical buildings, there is a really nice, shaded picnic area and this mission is the only one in California that has legit hiking. Each day at 1 p.m. they have a worthwhile docent-led walking tour that runs about 1.5 hours.

If you are only going to do one hike, check out the Cross Trail just behind the gift shop, which is a short uphill to the cross and offers expansive views of the mission and its surroundings. Another hike to consider is the easy/moderate 5–6 miler to the water tanks and back. If you're going to be on the hike past 5 p.m., make sure you park outside the gate of the mission so you're not locked in. Dogs are allowed (on leash). Bring water and a flashlight.

While this mission now is approximately 2,000 acres, back in the day, it was almost 300,000 acres and stretched all the way up toward SLO. Some of what you'll see on the grounds: a reconstructed blacksmith room, rooms for leatherwork, weaving, candle making, and carpentry, tallow vats, a grist mill, soldiers' quarters, a women's dormitory for unwed Chumash Indians older than 11, and two churches! If you become a fan of this mission like I did after visiting, check its website for special events they do throughout the year. The Sheep Shear Mission Life Day, Candlelight Tour, and Mountain Man Encampment are just some of the special days you can enjoy. Who wouldn't want to see how to shear a sheep with actual shears? I shear would.

Lompoc

Derived from the original name "Lum Poc" given by the Chumash from their language Purisimeño and meaning "stagnant waters" or "lagoon," and now pronounced LOM-Poke, this small town has more to offer than you might think. While going around town, keep an eye out for The Murals of Lompoc, which can be seen everywhere.

If you're hungry and need a pick-me-up, the best place to eat may be South Side Coffee Co., which is located right in the middle of town and has good coffee, bagels, sandos, etc. Another good option is the family-owned and -operated Sissy's Uptown Café, a local favorite that makes solid homemade meals, including soups, salads, quiches, sandos and cakes. They also have a full dinner menu and a bunch of great local wines. For a sando, head to Central Coast Specialty Foods. For the best woodfired pizza in town and big tasty juicy burgers, head to the Valle Eatery & Bar located at the Hilton Garden Inn. Angela's is known for good Mexican food. Head to Hangar 7 for a really cool wine and cocktail bar with great small plates to share, and a space theme that goes nicely with all the nearby space-related activities in Vandenburg.

For your afternoon activity, you should choose between wine tasting, the aquatic center, and the horse sanctuary.

Lompoc Wine Ghetto
Up next is the famed Lompoc Wine Ghetto located just north of Highway 246 between Seventh Street and 12th Street. I will admit that it took me more than seven years living on the Central Coast to make it to this region, and all I can say is, what a fail! This area is known for its pinot noirs, Bordeaux and Rhone's. In the lively industrial park, where most of the tasting rooms are located, you'll find

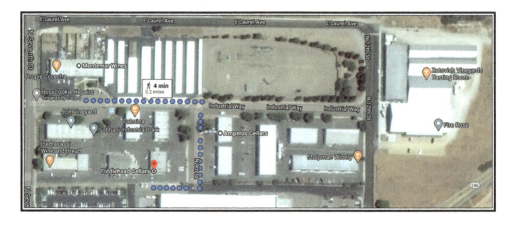

dozens of wineries serving up outstanding small batch wines. A few that never fail to please are Montemar Wines, Ampelos Vineyards and Cellars, Fiddlehead Cellars, and Taste of Santa Rita Hills. Ampelos was the first in the U.S. to be certified Organic, Sustainable and Biodynamic. The owners believe the care they take in their farming methods "makes its way all the way to your lips sip after sip." You'll need to be the judge of that. Fiddlehead gets special note because of its pioneering winemaker Kathy Joseph, who has been putting out delightful Sauvignon Blanc and Pinot Noir wines since 1989.

Lompoc Aquatic Center

If you brought kids along, perhaps skip some of the options above and head to the Lompoc Aquatic Center after lunch. With indoor pools and slides, your kids will love every second, but check the times as hours are strange and sporadic — some days it is only open from 1 to 3 p.m.

Dare 2 Dream Farms

Dare 2 Dream Farms in the southern part of town is the spot if you've been wanting a flock of chickens. If not, check out their farm stand and get yourself some free-range eggs.

Return to Freedom American Wild Horse Sanctuary

If you love horses, check out the highly praised Return to Freedom American Wild Horse Sanctuary. You'll need to make an appointment to visit or volunteer at https://returntofreedom.org/visit/.

Afternoon: At the beach?

Now that you've seen some of the town of Lompoc, head west, the ocean awaits! But wait, is it summertime? Then you cannot go to the beach! Early March until late September is Snowy Plover breeding season. Give these little cuties some privacy or get fined up to $5,000. Instead, skip the beach and head to the Burton Mesa Ecological Reserve (see below). During the rest of the year, you have two great beaches to choose from: Ocean Beach Park or Surf Beach. I say "great" because they are vast and CAN BE awesome! They also can be freezing with a capital BRRRRR! But you're not a wuss, so you have nothing to worry about. Just pull out your winter gear and windbreaker, and enjoy a walk along this really beautiful stretch of coastline.

Oddly, Surf Beach is where the Amtrak stops, and if you ever take the Amtrak through this area, you will wish this was your stop. Secluded beach in the middle of nowhere? Check!

Surf Beach

During very low tide, you can access some sea caves at the southern end of the beach. This beach is popular with bodyboarders and … you guessed it, surfers.

Ocean Beach Park is the mouth of the Santa Ynez River and is an estuary lagoon where all the watershed from the Santa Rita Mountains empties into the ocean. This is where to go if you want to see lots of birds. You might want to think twice about surfing here as there have been two fatal shark attacks. Notice any huge buildings on the horizon? Those are hangars for spaceships.

Ocean Beach Park

Burton Mesa Ecological Reserve

In the summertime, since you can't go to the beach, a great alternative is to check out the Burton Mesa Ecological Reserve. As one of the last remaining stands of maritime chaparral, and with more than 5,000 acres, you will have plenty of exploring to do. Bring binoculars for spotting birds and other wildlife. Leashed dogs are welcome. The Reserve is open sunrise to sunset daily.

Lompoc Flower Festival
The Lompoc Flower Festival from late spring to early fall is definitely worth putting in your calendar. See field after field blooming with every possible color. There are many flower varieties, including Bells of Ireland, delphinium, larkspur, stock, and sweet pea. If you've ever wanted to see the flower fields in Holland, save yourself the trip and head to Lompoc instead. The flower fields rotate every year, but you can normally find some on Central Avenue from Floradale to Union Sugar Avenue just west of Old Town Lompoc (downtown Lompoc). If you brought your bikes, you may want to ride them past all the fields. Keep in mind that these are private fields, so you are not allowed to walk through them.

Vandenberg Air Force Base
Once you're done in Lompoc, head north on Pacific Coast Highway, which will take you right past Vandenberg Air Force Base. Of course you've heard of Cape

Canaveral in Florida, but did you know that this is the place to be for West Coast rocket launches? If you are interested in space exploration, satellite launching or missile testing, you should reserve ahead and build your adventure around the once monthly "Windshield tour" on the third Tuesday at 1 p.m. Book a spot early as tours are limited to 30 people and fill up several months in advance. There is also a quarterly tour to the Space and Missile Heritage Center. See website for booking details: https://www.vandenberg.af.mil/Public-Tours/

This is a high-security facility so don't expect to see everything.

If you want to watch a spaceship launch, find the best view points and launch schedule at https://www.spacelaunchschedule.com/vandenberg-launch-schedule/. If you get in for either tour and you're coming from SLO, I suggest you make a morning of it beforehand in Santa Maria or Orcutt.

If you are not doing a tour of Vandenberg, continue north on PCH and, if you still have daylight, get ready for some stunning views of the surrounding rolling hills.

Dinner
To end your day, you might consider three possible dinner options that are more or less along the way home. If you like steak, ribs, beef or pork, you will love either The Hitching Post in Casmalia or Jocko's in Nipomo. My mouth begins watering every time I think of Jocko's. *Slocals Only* **pro tip**: If you are not a huge eater, share a meal, because you will still be stuffed. If you're a fan of seafood, Ada's Fish House in Pismo is the place for you.

EPIC Option: Skydiving
Do you want to make this **EPIC** day even more **EPIC** and create an everlasting memory? Skydive Santa Barbara (M-F 9-5p, Sat/Sun 8-6p) located in Lompoc is the only drop zone offering 18,000 ft jumps. That's three miles of falling and 90 seconds of free-falling while taking in coastal views, flower fields, wineries,

and space rockets! The standard jump is 13,000 feet with 60 seconds of free-falling. I have jumped out of a plane (in my 20s before I learned to fear things like dropping out of the sky) but haven't done it here. They've been in business for more than 30 years so, ya know, that means you're probably good. Grab a few friends and harness up for one of the most exhilarating things you'll ever experience. I suggest you do it first thing in the morning so you have the rest of the day to be happy to be alive. Enjoy!

Freefall with an ocean view in Lompoc

Santa Maria and Orcutt

Parks, Wine, Walks, and the Birthplace of Santa Maria Barbeque

What to Bring: hat, sunscreen, water, picnic, frisbees for disc golf, walking shoes, a large appetite
When to Go: Anytime
Duration/Distance: 4+ hours

Directions to Start: 101 South to Clark Ave, go west

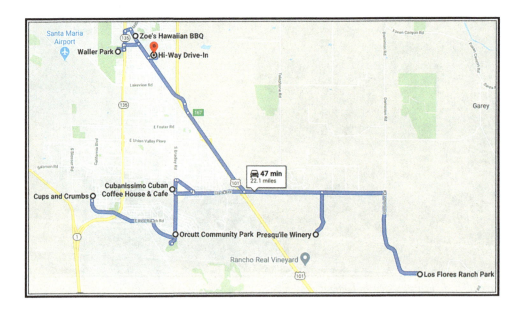

Thirty minutes south of SLO are a few towns that rarely get mentioned. I'll be the first to admit that when I think of adventure, Santa Maria and Orcutt don't immediately come to mind. However, if you give these towns a chance, you'll find more than enough for the adventurous to do in two days with several hidden gems. From great parks and wineries to yummy restaurants and one of only two drive-in theaters on the Central Coast, this area sees relatively few tourists and will feel off the beaten track.

Adventure Agenda	Option 1	Option 2
Breakfast	Cups & Crumbs, Kay's Orcutt Country Kitchen	Pure Natural Juice
Morning Adventure	Orcutt Community Park	Waller Community Park & either Museum of Flight or Discovery Museum
Lunch	Cubanissimo Cuban Coffee House & Café or The Far Western Tavern	Zoe's Hawaiian BBQ
Afternoon	Los Flores Ranch Park, Presqu'ile Winery	Horse sanctuary or Aquatic Center
Dinner	The Swiss Restaurant and Bar	Rancho Nipomo Deli & BBQ
Evening	Hi-Way Drive-in Theater	Pacific Conservatory Theatre

Orcutt

This unincorporated town located just south of Santa Maria in the Santa Maria Valley has a tight-knit community and a small, walkable downtown area referred to as "Old Orcutt." Start your day in Old Orcutt by taking the 101 south from SLO and taking exit 166 to Clark Street. Go west to "Old Orcutt" which is what the locals call the downtown area.

While not large by any means, Old Orcutt is a few cute streets with several murals and some fun shops. Grab some good coffee and breakfast at Cups & Crumbs. Or check out local favorite Kay's Orcutt Country Kitchen for its good eggs Benedict, Disney-themed pancakes, and other home-cooked breakfast staples.

After getting your fill, take a walk through the prime outdoor area in town, Orcutt Community Park.

Orcutt Community Park

Orcutt Community Park has several great walking trails that crisscross one another. To get your bearings, the main trail from the west side of the park is called Rice Ranch Trail and the main trail from the east side of the park is called Orcutt Hill Trails. For first-timers, Orcutt Hill Trails may be slightly better. This easy 3.1-mile loop has its fair share of walkers, runners, equestrians, mountain bikers, and dogs on leash. You'll get 301 feet of elevation gain and can add many side trips if you like. This is a great place to bring a picnic. Park near the roundabout and start by doing a simple loop around the sports fields, then head east (toward the end of the parking lot) and take the dirt trail which is a good meander through the hills.

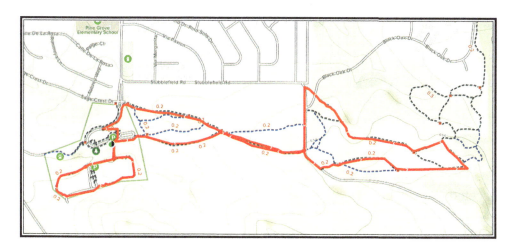

After finishing the Orcutt Hill Trails, if you'd like to add another 3.2 miles and 423 feet of elevation gain, head to the west side of the parking lot for Rice Ranch Trail.

If you didn't bring a picnic, you might want to swing by the Cubanissimo Cuban Coffee House & Café to grab a delicious sandwich prior to our next stop.

Orcutt Hill Trails

Los Flores Ranch Park

Located about 8 miles south of Santa Maria, this 1,778-acre property, located in the Solomon Hills, offers almost 8 miles of hiking, equestrian and mountain-biking trails. To get here, take Clark Avenue east from the 101 to Dominion Road. Go right (south) and you will see signs for the parking area. A good trail for first-timers is the East La Cuesta Loop, a 3.8-mile loop with 472 feet of elevation gain which takes you through some nice rolling hills with plenty of oaks and offers views in all directions.

Now its time to head to Santa Maria, where your next option awaits. Will be a park and planes, a park and interactive museum, or wine and then, who knows? I like to stop off at the lovely Presqu'ile Winery, off of Clark Avenue, to decide on what's next.

Santa Maria
Known for its wineries, namesake barbeque, and farming, this quiet town is by no means a draw for tourists, but has enough to keep you busy for a few daytrips thanks to its nice parks, walking trails, top-notch steakhouses, and some very remote nearby beaches. The annual Strawberry Festival in April offers more than 10 varieties of strawberries (who knew there were so many?) and everything strawberry related you could possibly want.

Waller Park

This park is huge! Located right in the middle of town, this varied and fun park offers many distinct areas and plenty of reason to get moving in any weather. There is a nice picnic area, multiple playgrounds for younger children, sports courts, ponds full of ducks and geese and good walking throughout. Bring your discs along since they have a really good disc golf course for all experience levels. If you are heading to this park instead of Los Flores Ranch Park, you should have lunch at Zoe's Hawaiian BBQ or for a healthier option, head to Pure Natural Juice for juice, smoothies, and sandwiches.

Santa Maria Museum of Flight

If you have young kids who like planes, they'll enjoy this museum, which is located very close to Waller Park. Open 10am–4pm Fri-Sun, this dusty and small museum has some really cool aviation related stuff and the free tour with one of the passionate guides will help the place come to life. Your kids will dig it!

Santa Maria Valley Discovery Museum

This interactive discovery museum is a fun stop if you have kids along for the adventure. Like many other discovery museums, kids get to touch, feel and sense their way through while learning something new. Can you hate it?

Dinner and a Show

After a full day of activities, since you are in Santa Maria, you have to eat Santa Maria-style barbeque. Well, you don't have to, but shouldn't you? This style of barbequing began back in the mid-1800s right here in Santa Maria and is even copyrighted by the Santa Maria Valley Chamber of Commerce. How is Santa Maria barbeque different than plain old barbequing, you might ask? To answer this, I went to the source of all great tri-tip knowledge: Wikipedia.

Santa Maria-style barbecue centers around beef tri-tip, seasoned with black pepper, salt, and garlic before grilling over coals of native coast live oak, often referred to as "red oak" wood. The grill is made of iron and usually has a hand crank that lifts or lowers the grill over the coals to the desired distance from the heat. The Santa Maria Valley is often rather windy, so the style of cooking is over an oxidative fire as opposed to a reductive fire that many covered barbecues use.

The traditional accompaniments are pinquito beans, fresh salsa, tossed green salad, and grilled French bread dipped in sweet melted butter.

By the late 1950s, three local restaurants—The Far Western Tavern, Hitching Post, and Jocko's were on their way to becoming landmarks of this style of barbecue.

If you want to stay in Santa Maria, a few spots where you can enjoy this culinary delight are The Swiss Restaurant and Bar, The Far Western Tavern (which will take you back to Old Orcutt), and the highly rated Rancho Nipomo Deli & BBQ. Not to start a war or anything, but for my money, the best Santa Maria-style barbeque is not in Santa Maria but in the nearby towns of Casmalia (Hitching Post) and Nipomo (Jocko's). They are all good, so why not give each a try and see who does SM-style BBQ best?

Once they roll you out of your dinner spot, it's time for a show and there are two fun options to finish your day: Hi-Way Drive in Theater or the Pacific Conservatory Theatre.

Hi-Way Drive-In Theater

At the time of publishing, this Drive-In was closed but "promised" to be re-opening soon. Cars start lining up 30 minutes prior to showtime, so get there early. They have a concession stand and/or you can bring your own snacks. Aside from the beloved Sunset Drive-in Theater in SLO, this  is the only other drive-in movie theater left on the Central Coast.

Pacific Conservatory Theatre

Believe it or not, there is a great theater based in Santa Maria. The PCPA - Pacific Conservatory Theatre has been putting on plays for more than 50 years. One of its most recent lineups included *Julius Caesar, Little Shop of Horrors, The Sound of Music*, and *The Little Mermaid*. Check their site (http://www.pcpa.org/) for shows and plan to book early so you get good seats. Plan your adventure to SM around a show.

EPIC Alternative for the Day

Scrap almost everything above, make a reservation at Jocko's, pack a picnic, and try this fun alternative to the day: Start your day walking in the Los Flores Ranch Park, then make your way east to do part of the Foxen Canyon Wine Trail. You'll be able to hit six wineries on the trail as you make your way north. Eat your picnic somewhat early so you'll have a large appetite. End your day with a feast at Jocko's. End your day with a feast at Jocko's and you too will be a fan of Santa Maria and Santa Maria-style barbeque.

Train Ride to Santa Barbara   36
Day Trip to One of the Most Beautiful Spots in California

What to Bring: hat, sunscreen, water, good walking shoes, picnic
When to Go: Any time of year
Duration/Distance: 3+ miles walking

Directions to Start: Amtrak station from SLO to downtown Santa Barbara

Adventure Agenda	Option 1	Option 2
Breakfast	At home/On train	Dawn Patrol
Morning Adventure	State Street (walking)	State Street (riding)
Lunch (and activity)	Public Market	Stearns Wharf - Santa Barbara Shellfish Company
Afternoon	Zoo or gardens	Bike ride along Shoreline Drive or kayak
Sunset/Dinner	Stearns Wharf - Santa Barbara Shellfish Company	Finney's Crafthouse

Oh, the romance of traveling by train. When that thought comes to mind, it evokes images of traveling effortlessly across the European countryside or even throughout the northeast. What most don't think about is the Pacific Surfliner hugging California's coastline and making stops in many of the major destinations. Yes, we are lucky enough to have an Amtrak station (https://www.pacificsurfliner.com/) right here in SLO that will take you south to Grover Beach, Guadalupe,

Lompoc, Goleta, and for the purposes of this adventure, Santa Barbara. That same Pacific Surfliner train can take you to Los Angeles or even all the way to San Diego. Oh, the places you'll go!

For this adventure, you will want to hop (or walk sleepily) onto the 6:55 a.m. train from the SLO station (check times as they may change). Sure, you could do this by car, but you'd be missing out on the joys of train travel on the central coast which hugs the coast and is absolutely lovely. Buy your train tickets online and have the ticket on your phone. Get seats on the west side of the train so you'll have front row seats of the beach in each direction. You'll be in Santa Barbara at 9:27 a.m. This is about an hour longer than driving, so you have time to watch a movie, read a book, or stare out the window as you rock your way down the coastline enjoying the fantastic ocean views.

Pacific Surfliner heading south towards Santa Barbara

The train back from Santa Barbara departs the station at 5:41 p.m. and arrives in SLO at 8:36 p.m. That gives you just over eight hours in Santa Barbara, which is perfect for a day trip. Clearly, staying a night in Santa Barbara so you have more time to explore is a good option.

Downtown Santa Barbara

Once you get off the train in Santa Barbara, you are conveniently located in the heart of this charming town, which was founded in 1786. Head straight for coffee and/or breakfast. The most convenient coffee shop is the Santa Barbara Roasting Company. It's right across from Amtrak, and also happens to be quite good! Directly across the street is a delicious breakfast spot, Dawn Patrol (which also has good coffee). For serious coffee snobs, you may want to hold out until you get to Handlebar Coffee Roasters. Santa Barbara has no shortage of good coffee, so you might also want to include stops at Dune Coffee Roasters or CAJE as part of your walk.

Assuming you've come to Santa Barbara for something other than coffee, you're in luck! You have many options for your day trip and should create the adventure that appeals most to you. You won't be able to do everything Santa Barbara has to offer in a day, so plan around the weather and what speaks to you most.

If you are a huge fan of Missions, you might call an Uber and go straight to Mission Santa Barbara, which is a little off the main drag, then walk back down State Street.

Mission Santa Barbara

Located downtown near State Street, this mission is one of the most beautiful missions in California. But is it worth your time on a day trip to Santa Barbara? For me, the answer is no since there is so much else to do and time is so limited. If, however, you have more than a day, you'll definitely want to check it out.

State Street

This is the main street of downtown Santa Barbara and the place to be if you're looking to do some shopping. This is the best shopping in the region; to get any better, you'd have to go to San Francisco or Los Angeles. Besides the popular chains you'd expect to see at any major mall (i.e., Apple, Banana Republic, H&M), there's also tons of local shops that feature goods from local artists, and a handful of consignment stores and antique shops. You'll have lots to see as you stroll up and down State Street. Depending on how slowly you walk up State Street, you could plan to eat at Public Market. If you're making pretty quick time, you should eat at Stearns Wharf.

Santa Barbara Public Market

This is the place to go if you are in a group where everyone wants something different to eat. This is my go-to stop if I start to get hangry around Santa Barbara while driving between Los Angeles and SLO (although I prefer the convenience of stopping in Los Alamos better). Visualize a gourmet food court and you have Public Market. There are new places all the time, but at the time of publishing they had: Empty Bowl (Asian/noodles), The Garden, Corazon Cocina, Enjoy Cupcakes, Rori's Ice Cream (organic ice cream), Wine + Beer (tasting room), Soul Cal BBQ, Ca'Dario Pizzeria

and Pasta. There was also a little market with a great assortment of food and snacks.

If you're not ready to eat yet, travel back down State Street toward the water. You might want to jut east over to Santa Barbara Boulevard to see the publicly accessible and very pretty Santa Barbara Courthouse. Then, as you continue down State Street, earmark Institution Ale — an extremely inviting, hipster brewhouse — for a drink later. Walk past the Amtrak station and keep going for Stearns Wharf. If you haven't eaten yet, my two picks for lunch are Finney's Crafthouse or the Santa Barbara Shellfish Company. Finney's Crafthouse is a great spot for pizza and craft beer. They have really good vegan options and gluten-free crust.

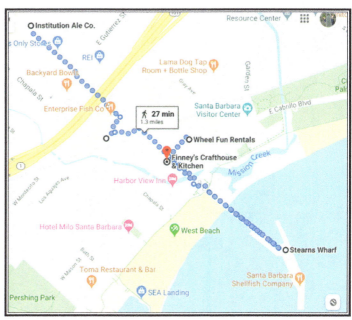

As you've already walked 2.5 miles, you might strongly consider a bike rental depending on what you want to do next. The beach is only about a quarter mile away and Stearns Wharf is 0.4 miles away, but if you want to go along the beach, you will easily add 1.5 miles in each direction. If you want a bike, head to Wheel Fun Rentals about a block south (toward the water) on State from the Amtrak, then go east on Mason. Otherwise, continue on to Stearns Wharf.

Stearns Wharf

The wharf and pier are a can't-miss stop on a trip to SB. This is the place to be if you want to eat with an ocean view. Santa Barbara Shellfish Company is calling your name if you want seafood, but expect a wait if you go right at mealtime. For all its "fame," there's not a whole lot to do on the pier except eat and gaze over the ocean or back at the lovely town of Santa Barbara. Take in the fresh, salty air and then move on to your next stop.

Train Ride to Santa Barbara

If you've been biking, you can ride to Shoreline Park (see next section for more information). Or, if you're walking, you can stop at Paddle Sports Center and rent a kayak or stand-up paddleboard to see the coast from the ocean. (In the event you're staying the night, you should strongly consider a paddle at sunset.) If on bike and you want to go to the Santa Barbara Zoo, now's the time. Head east from Stearns Wharf. By foot, get an Uber and head to the zoo or one of the local gardens.

Santa Barbara Shellfish Company

Shoreline Park

Take a lovely 1.5-mile walk or relaxing bike ride along the beach to Shoreline Park, a great place to lie in the grass, play frisbee, surf, watch the sunset, or have a picnic. There is access to the public beach from here and there's a great kiddie playground. It can be

windy here, so bring a jacket just in case. If you have a bike, you may want to continue west a few more miles to the Douglas Family Preserve, which is the largest coastal open space within Santa Barbara city limits.

Douglas Family Preserve

This 70-acre former nursery turned preserve (thank you, Michael Douglas!) has three miles of walking/running trails and gorgeous, undeveloped views of the Santa Barbara coastline. I suggest going here if you want to be a little more off the beaten path. If your time in Santa Barbara is limited to one day, I'd save this preserve for a future trip. However, combining a trip here with lunch or dinner at the Boathouse at Hendry's Beach, one of the most upscale and romantic spots in Santa Barbara, will be sure to impress your companions. Expect to wait if you show up at sunset. Plan ahead and make reservations here: https://boathousesb.com/reservations/

Moxi: The Wolf Museum of Exploration + Innovation

This highly interaction museum will keep kids of all ages entertained for hours. Located a short walk from the train station, this is definitely worth your time if you have young'uns with you.

Santa Barbara Zoo

This is one of the best midsized zoos on the West Coast. If you have kids in tow, you might skip some of the shopping and opt for the zoo and the Moxi instead. Once at the zoo, there is a train that runs around the perimeter of the zoo. Boom! Double down on trains. Can you hate it? No, you really can't.

If zoos make you feel all cagey, perhaps you'd prefer gardens instead? If so, Santa Barbara has your number. Uber to one of the following:

Santa Barbara Botanic Garden
This lovely garden, with more than 78 acres to explore, offers a great selection of local plants in themed areas. With so much ground to cover, you can get your hike in here while seeing and learning about hundreds of plant species. This is a special place for people of all ages. Make sure you check out the Mission Dam and Aqueduct along the Canyon Trail, built by the Chumash under direction from the Franciscan padres who ran the mission all the way back in 1806. The entrance fee is a bit steep, especially since this feels more like a hiking area and less like a garden than most visitors assume. You should try to plan your trip to coincide with spring so there will be more flowers.

Ganna Walska Lotusland
If you like plants, your mind will be blown when you visit Ganna Walska Lotusland, considered one of the best gardens in the world. But you really, really have to love plants because the entrance fee is $50 per adult! There are more than 20 gardens with different themes, including Aloe Garden, Water Garden, Blue Garden, Japanese Garden, Olive Garden with unlimited breadsticks (wait, that's somewhere else), etc. The garden is open Wednesday through Saturday from 10 a.m. to 4 p.m., but unless you sign up for membership, the only way to see the gardens are on a docent-led tour, which begins at 10 a.m. and 1:30 p.m. and lasts approximately two hours. You must reserve ahead of time at 805.969.9990. Late spring or summer offers more blooming flowers and is a good time to visit. Make sure you wear comfortable walking shoes.

Heading back downtown, check out the Santa Barbara Urban Wine Trail or a few of the many breweries.

The Santa Barbara Urban Wine Trail
Santa Barbara is known far and wide for great wines. Almost 30 wineries have tasting rooms conveniently located downtown or nearby and are collectively known as the Santa Barbara Urban Wine Trail. Some of the highest rated are Grassini Family Vineyards, Area 5.1, Municipal Winemakers, Skyenna Wine Lounge, Jamie Slone Wines, and DV8 Cellars. Deep Sea Winery is at Sterns Wharf, has a rooftop terrace, and is a great spot if you want to have a drink while watching the sunset. If you plan to visit more than three wineries and are open

about where to go, you'll save money by getting the Funk Zone Self-Guided Tour, which gives discounts and complimentary wine at several of the tasting rooms.

If beer is more your thing, then head for some of the great SB breweries.

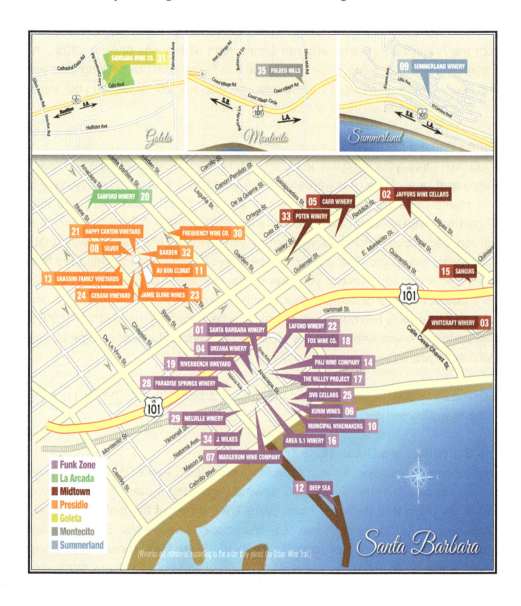

Santa Barbara Craft Beer

There is no shortage of breweries in SB, and if you're into the craft beer scene, you have plenty of options. One of the best is Figueroa Mountain Brewing Company. You'll also like Brass Bear Brewing and Bistro, Third Window Brewing, and Topa Topa Brewing Company.

But don't linger too long over that beer or wine — you have a train to catch! I'm assuming you've already drank your dinner, but perhaps you have time for a bite?

Downtown Dinner Spots
Santa Barbara is known for its restaurants and has something for everyone. Here are just a few of the very worthwhile options near the train station:

Finney's Crafthouse – Gastropub with American food and cocktail bar
Santo Mezcal – Mexican/Latin American food
Loquita – Tapas bar/modern European food
Blackbird – Mediterranean

Hop on your train back to SLO, get seats on the western (ocean) side, look out the window as the sun sets into the Pacific, and dream about your next trip down to lovely Santa Barbara. What a way to spend a day!!

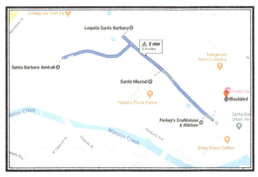

Christmas on the Central Coast

Fun Events Not-to Be Missed During October Through December

What to Bring: layers, jacket, gloves, beanie, your favorite toasty beverage in a thermos.
When to Go: Oct–Dec
Duration/Distance: Up to one hour driving each way and several hours to all day

Directions to Start: Varies depending on selected activity

The holiday period is a special time in the Central Coast, and much like the wildflower bloom in spring, if you happen to miss things by a day or forget to buy tickets, you'll be missing out. Events begin in October with the Scarecrow Festival in Cambria, and culminate with the Polar Bear Dip on New Year's Day in Cayucos. If you're lucky enough to be in the region during the right dates, plug them in to one of the other adventures for that area or create your own holiday adventure!

Holiday lights in Cambria

Below, I listed the days of the events so you have an idea of when they happen, but the actual day of most events change year to year. A few great resources that will help you keep things straight are enjoyslo.org and slocal.com.

October
Scarecrow Festival. Cambria. Oct 1-31

The Scarecrow Festival started in Cambria and now also includes San Simeon and Harmony. I like this festival because it's totally random — or "unique," as the festival website describes it. You will see scarecrows fishing, flying, painting, bathing, and flapping around on the beach. Wait, those are the elephant seals! This festival runs Oct 1-31.

Harvest (wine). Entire region. Late October

Late October also marks harvest for winemakers across the region. If you've ever wanted to stomp some grapes and learn about the winemaking process, here's your chance. Paso Robles has a ton going on and they do a great job keeping many of the events up to date here: https://www.pasorobleschamber.com/events.

Halloween October 31

Halloween in the area is really fun. Santa Margarita gets absolutely overrun with little ones. In SLO, the hottest spot for free candy from strangers is San Luis Bay Drive next to San Luis Obispo High School. In Paso, Vine Street is where you want to go. In many of the towns, you can support your local businesses while taking the kids to trick-or-treat. The shops downtown in SLO, Morro Bay, Paso Robles, and Atascadero all open up to the kids.

November
Cambria Christmas Market. Nov 23–Dec 23 (http://cambriachristmasmarket.com/)

This is not a market; this is a light show experience that spans many blocks. From 5 to 9 p.m. almost every night for a month, adults are impressed with how much work was spent on building the different light displays, and kids are amazed at the colors everywhere. This is a ticketed event and sells out every year. If you happen to be in the area, you shouldn't miss it. There is food and drink available at the

Cambria Christmas Market

event, including traditional German food like bratwurst. Drinks for sale include hot chocolate, coffee, and Glühwein, a traditional German mulled wine served warm.

Lighting Ceremonies. Late November

In late November, many of the Central Coast cities have lighting ceremonies. You can find one happening in Atascadero, Paso, Morro Bay, and SLO. Maybe I'm missing something, but I've never found these events to be all that exciting. Plenty of other people show up though, so to each their own.

City Park in Paso Robles

December
Non-Motorized Lighted Boat Parade. Morro Bay. Sometime in December

Christmas on the Central Coast

If you like boats and lights and Santas on stand-up paddle boards (SUP), and potentially drinking a beverage while watching said lighted boats and Santas on SUPs, you will love this event. The date is always TBD so check the Morro Bay website.

Madonna Inn Christmas Ambience. SLO. December

Any time in December is a great time to head over to the Madonna Inn for cake or a meal. Their regular food can't really hold a candle to their outrageous cake, but the holiday decorations in the main restaurant sure can. The staff spends weeks adorning the entire place with a display that is glorious in its eccentricity.

Madonna Inn at Christmas

Christmas Lights Parade. Paso Robles. Usually first week in December

http://www.pasoroblesdowntown.org

For nearly 60 years, this annual parade has helped spread joy across the land. Do not confuse this parade with the Victorian lights they have in Paso Robles about a week later; otherwise, like someone I know, you will be sitting in the cold watching floats go by when you really wanted to be walking around and keeping the blood flowing. However, if you are going to show up for the wrong event, this is a pretty good one to mistakenly attend.

South County Holiday Parade. Grover Beach 10–11am. Early December

For more than 50 years, this parade has been going strong and has the benefit of being the only daytime parade in south SLO county. The parade begins at 16th Street, travels west on Grand Avenue to 9th Street, and finishes at the Ramona Garden Park Center. Head over to the Ramona Garden Park Center to score some handmade goods at the Fine Art & Craft Faire that immediately follows the parade.

Holiday Musical Walk Around the Lake. Atascadero Town Lake. Early December

All the houses around the lake are lit up, there are over a dozen choirs, bell ringers, carolers, and other musicians all around the lake. The Atascadero Zoo is open for families, and on the lake walk there is hot cider, popcorn, and other refreshments available all free of charge.

Winter Wonderland. Atascadero. Early to mid-December

Who says the Central Coast doesn't have a white Christmas? During the Winter Wonderland event, they bring in literally tons of snow and create a snow slide and snow play areas. There are climbing walls, bounce houses, a train, *and* Santa and Mrs. Claus will be there. You can also find plenty to eat and drink at more than 50 local vendors. This is an extremely popular event and for good reason — it's awesome!

Vine Street Victorian Christmas Showcase. Paso Robles. Early to mid-December

One of my personal favorite holiday activities is to see almost every house from 8th through 21st Street decorated for Christmas. There is even one guy who dresses up like Scrooge and heckles passersby over a microphone. This is truly a spectacle and will definitely get you into the Christmas spirit. Oftentimes you can score some free cookies and hot cocoa. If you like Christmas at all, this is about as small town and Christmassy as you can get.

Scrooge lives on Vine Street

Polar Bear Dip. Cayucos. January 1

While some people love starting the year off hung over from partying too much the night before, others like to either kick it off with a bang or keep the party going until morning. Either way, running into the frigid Pacific with thousands of others who are going to take the New Year head-on is a rush and a memory that will last you a lifetime. The Polar Bear Dip is everything you need to wash the past year off of you and begin the New Year invigorated.

About the Author

Jared Friedman has called San Luis Obispo home since 2011. He lives here with his adventure-loving wife and two daughters. Jared has traveled to more than 30 countries and used countless travel guides along the way. Unable to find a guidebook about SLO that fully captured its beauty and fun, he was inspired to write his own.

Some of Jared's most notable adventures have been walking 500 miles across Spain (the Camino de Santiago), a three-day trek to the top of Mount Kenya, walking the Inca Trail to Machu Picchu, climbing and backpacking in New Zealand (he prefers the Routeburn Track to the Milford Track), sleeping on a felucca while sailing the Nile in Egypt, and RVing Iceland's Ring Road and the northwest fjords with two kids under the age of four. Oh, and doing a 30-mile, three-day, two-night backpacking trip on the Skyline Trail in the Canadian Rockies while he and his wife carried their two small girls, all their gear, and three days' worth of dirty diapers.

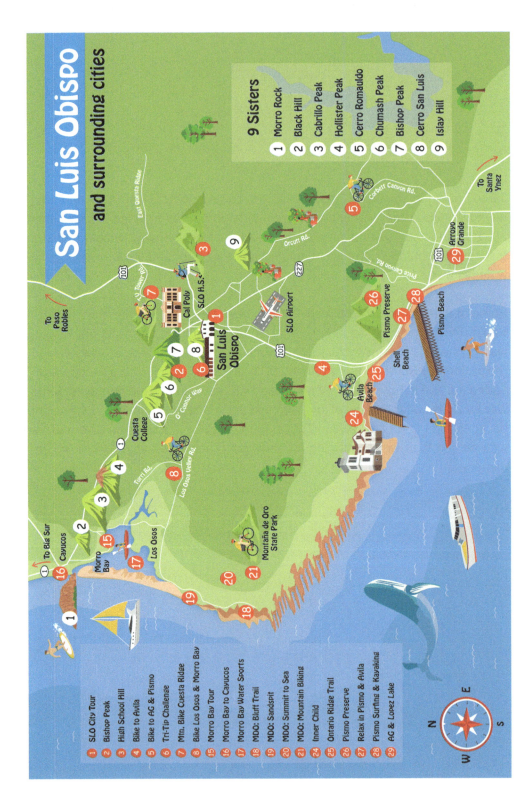

Made in the USA
Las Vegas, NV
17 October 2024

9700387R10167